D0028388

With the Nez Perces

UNIVERSITY OF NEBRASKA PRESS

LINCOLN AND LONDON

With the Nez Perces

Alice Fletcher in the Field, 1889–92

by E. Jane Gay

EDITED, WITH AN INTRODUCTION, BY
FREDERICK E. HOXIE AND JOAN T. MARK

Library of Congress Cataloging in Publication Data

Gay, E   Jane, 1830–1919.
  With the Nez Perces.

  1. Nez Percé Indians.   2. Fletcher, Alice Cunning-
ham, 1845–1923.   3. Gay, E. Jane, 1830–1919.   4. In-
dianists—United States—Biography.   I. Hoxie,
Frederick E., 1947–   II. Mark, Joan T., 1937–
III. Title.
E99.N5G39 1981   970.004'97 [B]   80–23045
ISBN 0–8032–3062–1

Contents

Illustrations

Preface

The book you are about to read is a unique document. It is a record of the adventures of two remarkable women and also a lens through which one can observe many of the forces and ideas that shaped American society in the late nineteenth century.

In 1889 the commissioner of Indian affairs appointed the anthropologist Alice C. Fletcher a special agent and sent her to Idaho to implement a new government program for the Nez Perce Indians. A friend from Washington, D.C., E. Jane Gay, accompanied Fletcher on the expedition. For the next three years they returned annually to Idaho, where they lived in tents and makeshift cabins while the anthropologist supervised the surveying of the Nez Perce Reservation and issued titles to an allotment of land to each member of the tribe. Jane Gay meanwhile kept house, took photographs, and wrote long letters to her friends back home. It is those photographs and letters that make up this volume.

Both the timing and purpose of their journey were dramatic signs of the changing relations between the United States government and Native Americans. The last military action between government troops and Indians—the massacre of Sioux men, women, and children at Wounded Knee, South Dakota—took place while Fletcher was engaged in the Nez Perce work. Some of the Nez Perces she met had themselves participated in Chief Joseph's war with the U.S. Army in 1877. The arrival of Alice Fletcher and Jane Gay on the tribe's reservation was another reminder that the era of armed conflict was coming to an end.

Moreover, Gay and Fletcher's expedition signaled a shift

in government policy. For a century, Native Americans had been considered aliens whose welfare was the exclusive concern of the federal government. They were "cleared" from the path of white settlement and forced to live on reservations, where they fell victim to the whims of inefficient (and often corrupt) Indian agents and the constant threat of new assaults on their diminished land base. By the late nineteenth century, this pattern of treatment had become intolerable, and the government turned instead to a program of forced assimilation. Alice Fletcher's task—to assign individual tribesmen to specific tracts of land—was part of that larger campaign to incorporate Indian people into the society that now surrounded them.

Jane Gay's letters and photographs therefore constitute a rare, first-person account of a critical event in Idaho and national history. But they are of interest for other reasons as well. Alice Fletcher and Jane Gay challenged their society's definition of what women should be and do. This account of their experiences, and Jane Gay's comments on the activities of the McBeth sisters, who were missionaries in Idaho, and on the lives of Indian women enlarge our perception of the role of women in American history. At the same time, the letters, which constitute a case study of one of the nineteenth century's great reform schemes, shed light on the reformers' motives and the consequences of their actions. And finally, Gay's letters provide a singular view of the Nez Perces, a people whose recent history remains largely unwritten.[1]

We gratefully acknowledge the cooperation, interest, and help of Patricia M. King, Director of the Schlesinger Library, Radcliffe College; Eva Moseley, Curator of Manuscripts, Schlesinger Library; Elizabeth B. Borden, formerly Director of the Women's Archives of Radcliffe Library (now the Schlesinger Library); James H. Davis, Photo Archivist, Idaho State Historical Society; and John Aubrey, Supervisor of Special Collections, The Newberry Library, Chicago. We have also made use of materials in the Harvard University Archives, the National Anthropological Archives at the

Smithsonian Institution, and the Idaho State Historical Museum, and of the Records of the Bureau of Indian Affairs in the National Archives. Gail Scho, Patricia Denault, and Mary Anne Causino assisted us with expert typing.

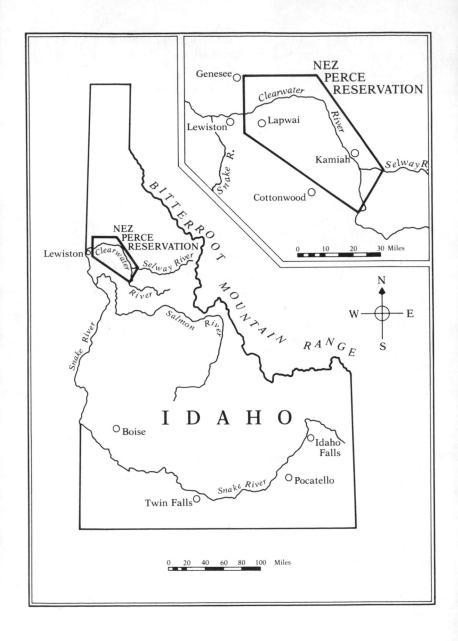

Introduction

Despite nearly three centuries of contact, it was not until the late nineteenth century that policymakers began to think seriously about ways to incorporate Indians into American society. Before the Civil War, both Congress and the Indian Office believed that most Native Americans should be kept separate from whites. The government's failure to maintain order on the frontier, as well as its commitment to westward expansion, convinced the nation's leaders that separation was the only way to avoid constant warfare. From this perspective, special federal preserves—reservations—appeared, to government policy makers, to be the best place for Indians to live. The reservation system evolved during these years and was soon the keystone of the nation's Indian policy.

But the reservation system soon lost its appeal. In the early nineteenth century, policy makers had believed there was enough land in the West for both expansion and reservations. No one could imagine the speed with which the territory beyond the Mississippi would be settled and organized into states. By 1870, with the Civil War over and the transcontinental railroad complete, the future looked quite different. The West was booming and the public no longer believed that reservations helped expansion by removing Indians from areas of settlement. Instead, reservations were seen as obstacles to the final "civilization" of the West. Suddenly, attacks on the reservation system began to come from every direction.

To western politicians, reservations were examples of federal meddling in the affairs of their new states and territories. They accused Washington policy makers of salving their own eastern consciences by dumping Indian refugees in unsettled areas and pampering these remnants of a race whose previous way of life they had participated in destroying. Farmers and railroad executives, encouraged by the government to treat the frontier as a blank canvas on which to paint their future, were outraged by laws barring them from reservations. Meanwhile, reformers shifted their concern from the black to the red man. Whether their goals were educational, religious, or legal, these apostles of Indian "uplift" found it impossible to accept the separation of Indians and whites. They believed Native Americans should be incorporated into the newly reunited nation and granted the benefits of the ballot, the public school, and a life that would allow daily contact with the "civilized" white majority. Reformers had varying objectives, but they were all agreed that the old philosophy of separation was no longer practical. They wanted to reduce the legal, economic, and cultural barriers between Indians and other Americans.

The General Allotment Act, sponsored by Massachusetts Senator Henry Dawes and signed into law by President Grover Cleveland in 1887, was the government's answer to mounting criticism of its reservation system. The new law marked the abandonment of separation and the beginning of a commitment to forced integration. It attacked the traditional tribal cultures of the Indians by attempting to instill in the red man the white man's concern for private property and individual achievement. The law had three main features. First, every Indian in the United States would receive title to a piece of land. Different categories of people would get different amounts (heads of households 160 acres, unmarried adults 80 acres, children 40 acres), but the intention was to provide every native family with a working farm. Second, since the Indian reservations contained far more land than would be needed for individual farms (the Indian population in 1880 was under 300,000 and "Indian country" consisted of more than 150,000,000 acres, or more than 500 acres per person), all "surplus" lands would be sold to the government and opened for settlement. Finally, every Indian who received an allotment would become an American citizen.

Economic, political, and social reform goals had been neatly combined.

Among the whites who welcomed the new legislation were merchants expecting an increase in westward migration, farm organizations looking forward to the availability of more land for settlement, and reformers who expected an early end to the corruption and stagnation of reservation life. The Indians, of course, were not consulted. Defined as backward, and lacking any significant political influence, they were left outside the policymaking process.

Historians have often been misled by the diverse parentage of the Dawes Act. Some writers have viewed the law as an idealistic document that fell prey to insensitive administrators and self-serving politicians. Others have seen the idealism of the measure as a transparent cover for greedy exploitation. Neither argument is correct, for the architects of the allotment law believed that assimilation and national expansion were entirely compatible. If the tribes resisted the new policy, it was because they did not appreciate the promise of American life or the bounty that lay before them. Although the transition to individual landownership might cause hardship or displacement, it would also bring education and civilization. And if whites profited from the new law, so much the better. Prosperity would promote good relations between the races and encourage the Indians to emulate their successful neighbors. In short, the Dawes Act's supporters argued, any temporary suffering would be overcome by the economic development of the West. They promised Native Americans a smaller piece of a larger, richer pie.

The severalty law established a new basis for the nation's Indian policy. It was the first piece of general Indian legislation in more than half a century. Yet it was supposed to be put into effect slowly, at the discretion of the president. "Reservations should be taken first," advised the Indian Rights Association in one of its pamphlets, "which are ripest for the work, where the way is clear, the risks small, the complications few." Commissioner of Indian Affairs John Atkins noted in his annual report for 1887 that too great haste should be avoided in the application of the law.[1] It would be applied on a case-by-case basis, presumably beginning with the tribes that were most eager for individual landownership. Atkins's report contained a list of twenty-five reservations where the government believed attitudes were "generally favorable" to allotment. One of those was the Idaho home of the Nez Perces.

The Nez Perces, who call themselves *Nimipu*, first came into contact with Anglo-Americans—members of the Lewis and Clark expedition—in the fall of 1805. As he foraged ahead of his companions, William Clark had left the eastern slope of the Bitterroot Mountains and descended across the plateau above the Clearwater and Snake river valleys. First he encountered some children, then a small group of families. These were the Nez Perces. They welcomed Clark and fed both him and the companions who straggled in later that day. Meriwether Lewis and the rest of the party were soon assembled, and together they traveled with the Indians to the nearby settlement of Kamiah on the floor of the Clearwater valley. There they rested, gathered information about the best route to the Pacific, and prepared themselves for the final leg of their journey. The Nez Perces promised to look after the explorers' horses and heavy equipment while the group floated down the Snake and Columbia rivers to the coast. The expedition departed in October and returned the following spring.

In 1806, before leaving the Clearwater country for their return trip to St. Louis, Captain Lewis recorded that the Nez Perces were "among the most amiable men we have seen. Their character is placid and gentle, rarely moved into passion, yet not often enlived by gayety."[2] The tribe's reputation for friendliness began with this visit. But there was more to the Indians' reaction than simple hospitality, for the Nez Perces saw the Americans as potential allies in their struggle to survive in an increasingly dangerous and hostile environment.

Traditionally, the Nez Perces lived in scattered villages and maintained few tribal institutions. Their aboriginal homeland, the western slope of the Rockies, was marked by high plateaus and deep river valleys. Tribal life revolved around small, semipermanent villages that lay along the shores of the major streams and creeks. Each village contained ten to seventy-five people, and there may have been as many as three hundred villages in the Snake, Wallowa, Clearwater, and Salmon river valleys. These were winter camps and the sites of spring salmon harvests. In the summer and fall, Nez Perce families abandoned their villages and gathered roots and berries on the plateaus or hunted for large game in the nearby mountains. Because their survival required that the tribe move in this annual cycle and spread itself thinly across the countryside, the Nez Perces had no permanent settlements and no political organizations with authority over the entire group. They supported village councils and followed local headmen, but their national identity derived principally from their common language and religious beliefs.[3]

We cannot know when the Nez Perces first felt the effects of the European invasion of North America. Perhaps the smallpox epidemics that crossed the plains in the eighteenth century reached them. Perhaps they learned of the whites when they acquired their first horses in the 1750s and began crossing the Bitterroots to hunt buffalo with the Crows. They may have remained oblivious to the newcomers until the Hudson's Bay traders brought them knives and rifles in the decade just prior to Lewis and Clark's journey. But whatever the answer, it was clear by 1805 that the tribe knew its traditional world had been disrupted. Lewis reported that the Indians he encountered along the Clearwater were "by no means so much attached to baubles as the generality of Indians, but are anxious to obtain articles of utility, such as knives, tomahawks, kettles, blankets and awls for moccasins. They have also suffered so much from the superiority of their enemies that they are equally desirous of procuring arms and ammunition, which they are gradually acquiring."[4]

Obviously the tribe was aware of the power and utility of trade goods. And their concern was understandable, since the intrusion of European cultures into their lives threatened a number of their traditional practices. Village headmen and civil authorities felt inadequate to control events or advise their people concerning the strangers that now appeared among them. Military leaders feared for their ability to repel aggressive tribes like the armed and mounted Flatheads and Shoshones. And shamans were pushed to the limits of their knowledge when they tried to understand or turn back the tide of new diseases. In each of these areas previously accepted methods failed the Nez Perces. Beset by these pressures and lacking a strong political system, the tribe began breaking into competing factions. Local headmen and groups of villages allied themselves with a variety of outsiders in an effort to improve their position and preserve a cultural identity. Throughout the nineteenth century, travelers like Lewis and Clark, missionaries, and government officials were seen by tribesmen as potential resources. By drawing on the power of these non-Indians, the Nez Perces hoped to overcome some of the forces assaulting them. The explorers were a source of weapons and tools. Others offered different things, but each new group appealed to a faction within the tribe. The result was usually confusion regarding the Indians' motives and the persistent fragmentation of traditional life.

In the early years of contact with non-Indians, the tendency to tap the resources of outsiders had little impact on the structure of the tribe. Warriors and headmen befriended various trappers and secured what advantages they could. But in 1836, the Nez Perces began a new relationship that produced some permanent changes. That year a group of Presbyterian missionaries arrived in Idaho and settled in the heart of Nez Perce country. They had been invited to the Northwest by a delegation from Kamiah that had traveled to St. Louis five years earlier. While the Presbyterians had taken the village's invitation as a providential sign, they soon realized that the Indians had been seeking something more than spiritual salvation. One of the early missionaries wrote that the Nez Perces "seem to wish to make the [mission] stations their trading posts, and the most they want of us is to supply them their temporal wants."[5]

But the Presbyterians were not traders; they built permanent homes among the Nez Perces and devoted themselves to converting members of the tribe. The result was the fragmentation of the Indian community. The leaders at Kamiah and the mission settlement near Lapwai were usually cooperative and friendly to the Christians, while the headmen from more remote areas, such as the Snake and Salmon river valleys, stayed away from the church and earned the name "heathen." These divisions were amplified in the 1840s when white settlers began streaming into the Oregon country, and the missionaries failed to oppose their encroachments. Although tensions at Lapwai never produced the kind of violence that took place at the Whitman mission in the present state of Washington, the Christian and "heathen" factions within the Nez Perce tribe drifted farther and farther apart. Each became convinced that the other was a threat to the tribe's well-being.

At mid-century, when the Indian Office began moving Indians in the Northwest onto reservations to separate them from the growing white population, religious differences within the tribe began to take on political significance. The Nez Perces signed their first treaty with the United States in 1855. This agreement called for no land cessions, but it required the tribe to recognize the authority of the American government and to accept the imposition of the office of principal chief onto their political system. The first principal chief was Hal-lal-hot-soot, also called The Lawyer, who was the leader of the Christian faction within the tribe and headman at Kamiah (the settlement that had welcomed Lewis and Clark in 1805 and sent to St. Louis for missionaries in 1831).

Lawyer was a classic example of the local chief determined to use his ties with the Americans to enhance his own standing within the tribe. While the "heathens" from the Salmon and Wallowa river valleys considered him a figurehead, he used his position to protect his followers and mediate between the Nez Perces and the government. The two factions finally parted company, and thereby split the tribe, in 1863.

The decision to dissolve their tribal ties occurred after the Indian Office announced its intention to negotiate a new treaty with the Nez Perces. The proposed agreement called for the sale of a large portion of the reservation. The hope was that the new cession would satisfy white land hunger and guarantee peaceful relations between the Indians and the new Territory of Idaho. Lawyer and his followers lived in the only section of the old reservation that would remain undisturbed by the proposed treaty. They readily accepted it. But most of the leaders of the "heathen" faction were slated to lose their homes and were unalterably opposed to the government's plan. Faced with this impasse, the two groups decided to separate. The anti-treaty party, led by Old Joseph and White Bird, returned to their villages while the Lawyer faction signed the agreement. Since the government recognized Lawyer as the principal chief of the Nez Perces, it declared that all the tribesmen were bound by the new accord.[6]

The rejection of the 1863 treaty by the leaders of the Wallowa and Salmon valley groups led directly to the tragic war of 1877. After 1863 the anti-treaty villages became increasingly anti-white and anti-Christian. They sought out allies other than the Anglo-Americans and found new ways to preserve their culture and combat the influences of the outside world. Their principal weapon in this effort was a nativist cult which taught the importance of retaining tribal lands and the power of traditional spirituality.[7] These lessons had great appeal in the "hostile" villages and became an important source of group solidarity. Meanwhile, Lawyer and his group took exactly the opposite tack—they cooperated with the Indian Office and turned in growing numbers to Christianity.

In the spring of 1877, after years of inconclusive negotiations, the government made a determined effort to enforce the 1863 treaty. Hostile leaders, who had continued to live in areas now considered off the reservation, were called to meet with General O. O. Howard at Lapwai. Howard, a Civil War veteran who had won fame for his work among former slaves (Howard University was named for him), insisted that the "hostiles" select land within the new boundaries and move onto the reservation. The group's leaders agreed to Howard's demands, but before their resettlement was complete a band of young men attacked some local white settlers. Panic gripped both Indians and whites; the cavalry was mobilized, and the anti-treaty faction fled into the mountains.

During the next four months, Chief Joseph, along with his brother Ollokut and the war chief Looking Glass, led their fellow tribesmen (and General Howard) on a circuitous retreat through the Rockies and across Montana toward the Canadian border. Their journey ended only a few miles short of their goal. Surrounded by a superior force and fearful that the coming winter would kill most of his people, Joseph appeared under a white flag. In his famous surrender speech he promised that he would "fight no more forever."[8]

The Indian Office condemned the hostiles for their recalcitrance, and the government continued its efforts to "civilize" the tribe. The majority of the Nez Perces had stayed on the reservation during the fighting and refused to cooperate with Joseph. The war furthered the process of tribal fragmentation that had begun with the arrival of the Presbyterians. As Joseph and his followers became more opposed to the government, those who sided with the Indian Office became more attached to their teachers and missionaries. Moreover the defeat of Joseph's followers and their subsequent confinement on a reservation in Indian Territory (present Oklahoma) left the Christian segment of the tribe in complete control of the reservation. At the end of the Nez Perce fighting the tribe's agent, John Monteith, reassured his superiors in Washington that the Indians remaining on the reservation had made "commendable progress." Referring to the settlement at Kamiah, he added that "no tribe of Indians can be found who have made the progress that these Indians have made during the past six years."[9]

But Agent Monteith, like Meriwether Lewis before him, saw only a portion of the truth. The remaining members of the tribe rejected the warpath in 1877 not out of love for the white man, but because they believed accommodation would better serve their ends. Factionalism continued to persist on the reservation in the postwar period. Tribal divisions continued to emerge as a consequence of pressure from advancing whites, and membership in the major groups continued to be a function of village affiliation. At the eastern end of the reservation many tribesmen looked to the Presbyterian church as an instrument for maintaining their identity and position. These people focused their attention on the congregations at Kamiah and other small towns and on the young Nez Perce men who were beginning to fill their pulpits. Some of these, like Archie Lawyer, were related to earlier leaders of the treaty party, while others, like Robert Williams, were men who had risen to positions of influence as a result of their education and conversion to Christianity.

On the west side of the reservation (near the agency headquarters at Lapwai) most of the village headmen relied on the government for protection and assistance. An agent like John Monteith had broad powers on the reservation. He could prosecute—or overlook—liquor selling and backstairs agreements with local white ranchers. He could provide people with government jobs (such as a position on the tribal police force), and he supervised the annual distribution of food and annuity payments. Many of the tribesmen who gravitated to the agent were from villages where the local minister had not yet displaced the traditional headman and where there was a greater tolerance of nonbelievers. Yellow Bull, for example, who had ridden with Joseph in 1877, settled near Lapwai when the government permitted him to return to Idaho and became associated with the group that came to be known as the "agency crowd."

As in the past, each of these new groups within the tribe believed itself to be the proper guardian of the Nez Perce future. Because the reservation was so large and the Indians so dispersed, the factions could generally live in a state of peaceful coexistence. But when the government called a tribal council, or some other event brought them into contact, their differences became clear. The tribe's annual celebration of the Fourth of July was one of those occasions. Each summer the Lapwai group welcomed the national holiday as an opportunity to enjoy horse racing, dancing, and the other activities that traditionally had been a part of the mid-year camas harvest. The Presbyterians at Kamiah, on the other hand, condemned the gambling that inevitably accompanied those races and would not tolerate ceremonies reminiscent of their "heathen" past. The two groups spent the day separately, while attacking each other for betraying the tribe. These verbal assaults sometimes led to more serious confrontations. In 1879, for example, a group from Lapwai suddenly rode into the midst of Kamiah's holiday celebration. The Presbyterian Nez Perces were about to begin a church service. "As the procession . . . to the grove where the [religious] exercises were held began," the agent later reported, "those wearing blankets and holding to Indian costumes attempted to join in such party, but were at once ordered out by the chiefs and elders." [10]

When Alice Fletcher and Jane Gay arrived at Lapwai in June 1889, they found the Indians living near the agency to be uncooperative. Few on the reservation spoke out against the Indian Office and its programs, but most tribal members were far from eager for the "progress" allotment promised. The Indians continued to spend most of the year in their small villages along the Clearwater and its tributaries. They maintained their primary allegiance to village headmen, whether those people were Christian ministers or traditional elders. And they persisted in thinking of themselves as *Nimipu*, a people with values and interests of their own. Much had changed in the tribe's way of life during the nineteenth century, but many of their traditional ideas and practices had survived.

The persistence of Nez Perce culture amid divisions within the tribe is the background against which Jane Gay's letters were written. That background explains Alice Fletcher's initial frustrations with the leaders at Lapwai and her warm reception at Kamiah. There, in the Presbyterian stronghold, her program could be perceived as a way of combating the "agency crowd" back at Lapwai. People might accept allotment for what it would do for their standing in the tribe rather than for its other, heavily advertised advantages.

Throughout their four-year assignment, Alice Fletcher and Jane Gay were continually faced with people who did not view allotment as they did. They had difficulty understanding that there were those who did not share their faith in the Dawes Act. To the two women, the law seemed to promise the Indians a measure of security in the years ahead. "One would expect," Jane Gay wrote in 1890, "that the young men who have for years been under the enlightening influence of the governing centre of the reservation would be able to see that treaties are abrogated by the logic of events." Instead the Nez Perces, both those who sided with Fletcher and those who did not, continued to pursue their own goals. They cooperated with outsiders when it suited their ends. And these outsiders, following in the footsteps of Meriwether Lewis, the Presbyterian missionaries, General Howard, and Agent Monteith, continued to be perplexed.

The last of Jane Gay's letters was dated September 6, 1892. By that time Alice Fletcher had made nearly two thousand allotments on the reservation. All that remained was for the Nez Perces to approve the sale of the 500,000 acres of tribal land that were not needed for their homesteads. The Dawes Act provided that the legacy derived from this property be used for the benefit of the entire group. The negotiations leading to the sale of this land constituted the final act in the internal political struggle of the allotment years.

Opposition to the land sale centered in the same Lapwai group that had originally opposed Fletcher's work. These people realized that without tribal lands there would be no tribal police, no tribal courts, and no agency patronage. "It was plainly evident," the Nez Perce agent wrote, "that the emoluments derived from the present state of the reservation would be entirely cut off . . . if the surplus lands were disposed of."[11]

Despite the cogency of their appeal, opponents of the sale were overcome by the group that had allied itself with the allotting agent. James Reuben, whom Fletcher had won over to the scheme, led the supporters of the land sale. "I have not many cattle or horses," he explained to the council that gathered to decide the issue. He hoped that the proceeds of the land sale would help him make a start as a farmer. "I wish to take a course which will lead to my benefit and that of my people," he told them, adding, "I don't think I should be benefited if left empty-handed with reference to the country unallotted."[12] The tribe approved the sale in March 1893, and in 1895 all unallotted reservation land was opened to the public for homesteading.

Although the income from the surplus lands brought a few years of prosperity, the long-term effects of allotment were disastrous. By 1902 thirteen towns and twenty post offices had been established on the old Nez Perce Reservation. "The changes this produced," a modern anthropologist has written, "were greater than any that had taken place before."[13] Bootlegging became a common crime and alcoholism a major problem. The arrival of commercial agriculture made traditional lifeways based on hunting and subsistence farming obsolete. And with little experience as farmers, people in the tribe increasingly exchanged the uncertain income of that occupation for the security of the *rentier*. With hundreds of whites eager to cultivate the Indians' holdings, the agency modified its rules prohibiting the leasing of individual homesteads. By 1911 fully 98 percent of the 136,000 acres of allotted land on the former reservation had been rented.[14]

Disease also continued to stalk the tribe. Tuberculosis was their principal curse, but other infectious and dietary diseases were also evident. Barely fifteen years after Jane Gay wrote that the question of whether their work had been beneficial must remain "among the unsolvable," the tribe's agent predicted, "It will be only a few generations before the tribe is extinct."[15]

Extinction did not occur. Allotment brought the tribe a period of intense suffering and change, but its identity remained intact. Its reemergence as a political unit began in 1923 when James Stuart, Alice Fletcher's interpreter during the allotment years, became the first president of the Nez Perce Home and Farm Association. This group formed the basis for a tribal council that was organized in 1927. The divisions within the tribe that Jane Gay had described in 1889 continued to dominate its internal politics, but the strength of this new institution has grown steadily. In recent years, the Nez Perces, like so many other groups that were ravaged by allotment, have devoted much of their energy to the cultural and economic reconstruction of the tribe.[16]

Jane Gay (1830–1919), whose visits to the Nez Perces between 1889 and 1892 resulted in the letters and photographs collected here, traveled widely during her life. Yet she always thought of herself as a Yankee "of Scottish descent" whose greatest virtues were the New England ones of forthrightness, frugality, and a practical turn of mind. She also had a penchant for reflection and a sense of humor, qualities much in evidence in these letters.

Jane Gay was born in Nashua, New Hampshire, the second child in a large family. After receiving an unusually good education for a girl in her time, including study with the pioneer female educator Emma Willard at Troy, New York, she went south with a friend to teach, first at the East Tennessee Female Institute in Knoxville, Tennessee, and later in Macon, Georgia. When the Civil War began, she moved to Washington, D.C., and worked with Dorothea Dix nursing wounded soldiers.[17]

Next she tried a literary career, publishing in 1868 under the pseudonym Truman Trumbull a book-length narrative poem about the Civil War, *The New Yankee Doodle*. Around 1871 Jane Gay took a job as clerk in the Dead Letter Office ("seventeen years in the penitentiary," as she later put it)[18] and became a member of the Washington social set called the "cave-dwellers." The "cave-dwellers" were long-term residents of Washington, D.C., in the area around Lafayette Square. Their members included leading figures in Washington art, government, and scientific circles, and the tone of the group was set by Mr. and Mrs. Henry Adams. In general they considered themselves cultured first citizens and disdained the flamboyant and "vulgar" new wealth that was moving into the nation's capital.[19]

Sometime during the 1880s Jane Gay and Alice Fletcher chanced to meet at a public lecture in New York City and renewed a friendship begun some forty years earlier when they had both been students at a girls' boarding school in Brooklyn and Fletcher, "little Alice," had been the youngest child in the school.

Jane Gay's sympathies were once again aroused by "little Alice," now a short, plump, modest-appearing woman who spoke quietly and walked with a limp (the result of an attack of inflammatory rheumatism while working on the Omaha Reservation in 1882) but who was a formidable force in the Indian reform movement and increasingly respected as a scientist. Jane Gay's name begins to appear in Alice Fletcher's diary for 1888, in brief but frequent entries: "Ill in bed but gaining . . . Miss Gay like a mother" and "Miss Gay kindness itself."[20] Jane Gay was concerned that her friend was not eating well or taking care of herself on her government assignments in the field. When the Nez Perce assignment came, Gay decided to go with Fletcher, to cook and keep house, and also to try out the still relatively new art of photography.

Alice Fletcher had not entered upon her career as an anthropologist and government agent until she was in her forties. Born in Cuba, where her parents had gone in a vain attempt to restore her father's health, Alice Cunningham Fletcher (1838–1923) was the daughter of a New York lawyer and a "Boston lady." She was educated in the best schools available, and then taught and was active in the temperance, anti-tobacco, and feminist movements. It was the sudden need to earn her own living that propelled her first into a career as a public lecturer and then into anthropology. While gathering material for her "Lectures on Ancient America," Fletcher met Frederic W. Putnam, the director of the Peabody Museum of Archaeology and Ethnology in Cambridge, Massachusetts, and began to study archeology informally with him. In 1881 her interests turned to contemporary Indians when she met two young Omahas, Susette and Francis La Flesche, in Boston, and arranged to travel with them to Nebraska, where she would camp and observe Indian life.[21]

Over the next several years Alice Fletcher turned herself into a professional anthropologist. Putnam had taught her the importance of scientific study in archeology, which to him meant painstaking and thorough excavation of bones and artifacts with detailed record keeping on where and in what condition the objects were found. Alice Fletcher transferred Putnam's emphasis on getting the facts to her new field, ethnology. She invented a new approach to the subject, the rigorous, first-person study which came to be called doing field work. As she traveled among the Plains Indians, she participated in their life and took detailed notes on their customs and ceremonies. Throughout the 1880s she presented papers based on her observations at the meetings of the American Association for the Advancement of Science or published them in the annual reports of the Peabody Museum.[22]

Simultaneously she became a leader in the growing campaign for the reform of the reservation system. Fletcher had met Susette and Francis La Flesche while they were on a speaking tour in the East with Standing Bear, the Ponca chief, protesting the removal of the Poncas to Indian Territory and calling for the extension of citizenship to Native Americans. When she got to Nebraska, Alice Fletcher learned that the Omahas were afraid they too might be banished from their homes. Joseph La Flesche, Susette and Francis's father, and some of the other leaders of the tribe had built frame houses and begun to farm on the reservation, but they were afraid that the government would abolish their reservation and move them elsewhere to keep them away from white settlers. The Indians wanted individual legal title to their farms, just as the white men had. Alice Fletcher listened sympathetically to their story and took up their cause. She lobbied in Washington for the passage of a special act which provided for the division of the Omaha Reservation into individual allotments of land. When the Omaha allotment act was passed in 1882, she was sent by the Bureau of Indian Affairs to Nebraska to implement it. Her work was so thorough that the bureau next hired her to make a nationwide survey of all the Indian reservations, their history, current situation, and the educational facilities available on each for helping the Indians toward "civilization."[23] With the completion of that report, Fletcher began to be recognized as one of the foremost authorities on Indians in the country.

She continued to lobby in Washington for a general allotment act. She also raised money for Indian education and home building and took an active part in the annual meetings of the Lake Mohonk Friends of the Indian, a reform group which urged the government to abandon the reservation system and promote the rapid integration of Indians into white society. When the Dawes Act was passed, Fletcher was sent to make the land allotments to the Winnebagos, a small group situated near the Omahas in Nebraska. Then came the more difficult assignment, to go to the more numerous Nez Perces in Idaho.

Alice Fletcher is "Her Majesty" in these letters, so called by her friends because of her resemblance to Queen Victoria but also perhaps as a humorous way of acknowledging the great respect approaching awe they were beginning to feel toward her. She is also occasionally the "Measuring woman."

Jane Gay appears in her own letters alternately as "she," the sensible cook, and as "he," the philosophical photographer, a division of roles which gave full expression to the two sides of her character but which also was probably intended as an ironic comment on her status within the group.

Jane Gay was familiar enough with Washington to know that artists and photographers had frequently been official members of government survey parties. John K. Hillers, William Henry Jackson, Thomas Moran, and T. H. O'Sullivan had all gotten their start or at least been active participants in western explorations. Jane Gay spent the summer of 1888 learning photography at the home of her brother Ziba Gay and his family at North Chelmsford, Massachusetts, in the hope that she would then be named an official member of the party. That fall she spent a month with Fletcher at the Winnebago Agency taking careful photographs of Omaha practices and artifacts, such as demonstrations of skin scraping and examples of beadwork.[24]

But the Bureau of Indian Affairs was much less inclined toward disinterested research than the old geographical and geological surveys had been. Jane Gay was not made an official member of the party. She had to be content with her unofficial status, and her reason for traveling to the far west became her kitchen activities. Henceforth she was free to photograph when and what she liked, with the result that the quality and interest of her photographs increased greatly.[25] At the same time, however, the activity itself was devalued, turned into an amateur's pastime. Jane Gay seems to have taken photographs mainly to amuse her family and friends. So little did she value the results of her work that she left the plate glass negatives in Idaho, where they were stored in the attic of the Lapwai mission house.[26]

In calling herself "he" as photographer, Jane Gay is perhaps indicating her feeling that only male photographers were taken seriously. Yet the act of photographing was clearly important to her, even if it had only the status of a hobby. It was a way of catching the details of life which she valued. It also enabled her periodically to step outside the everyday domestic routine. It brought a time of forced detachment that allowed her to reflect on the allotting party's situation. The conclusions she came up with were sometimes as refreshing and original as Jane Gay herself.

What did E. Jane Gay think of the work that they were in Idaho to do? Alice Fletcher was convinced that the allotment policy was a good thing for the Indians. She respected "the old ways," and indeed she was to spend most of the rest of her life documenting them, but she believed they were gone forever, as assuredly as were the buffalo on which so much of Plains Indians life had come to be based. The only hope she saw for the Indians was for them to become assimilated into white society and to take on "civilization."

Fletcher's convictions were the combined result of her experiences among the Omahas and the influence of the theory of social evolution set forth by Lewis Henry Morgan in *Ancient Society* (1877). Morgan had suggested that human societies everywhere evolved through developmental stages from savagery to barbarism to civilization. He believed that most American Indians were still at the level of Lower or Middle Barbarism, from which in time they would move up to Civilization. It was changes in the arts of subsistence which, above all, prodded groups from one level to the next, although there were concomitant changes in family structure, forms of government, and ideas about property. Fletcher believed that she was helping this necessary and inevitable process along, and she worked at it from every direction, forcing the Nez Perces to give up hunting and gathering to become farmers, urging them to break tribal ties and give their allegiance to federal, state, and local governments, and encouraging a strong sense of private property and above all the responsibility of the individual to better himself and his family. The frequent reference in these letters to "barbarism" and "civilization" are reflections of Morgan's theory.

Although Jane Gay in general agreed with her friend, she went west with considerably less ideological fervor than Alice Fletcher had by 1889 acquired. She could see clearly and sometimes commented wryly on the cost of "civilization" for the Nez Perces. She was aware that the struggle in which they were engaged was a poignant one and the outcome not at all clear.

But Jane Gay had too much respect for her friend's authority to challenge her, and so she remained an onlooker. Her general attitude was one of detachment. The allotment program was not her policy. She was not in charge. Her sphere was the housekeeping and as much photography as she cared to do. Only twice did Jane Gay try to take a more active role in the scientific and political activities which were her friend's province. The first was her brief career as an archeologist (see Letter Twenty-three), which was a failure in her own eyes, one senses, because "Her Majesty" did not take it seriously and encourage further attempts. The second was her intervention in the Fourth of July celebration in 1891.

"Talmaks," the Nez Perce combination of Fourth of July celebration and Presbyterian camp meeting which is described in Letter Twenty-two, had a complex and emotionally tinged history, not all of which Jane Gay understood. The missionaries had encouraged Fourth of July celebrations modeled on those of small-town America, with picnics and speeches. Under their sponsorship, these became, in effect, camp meetings, held annually both at Kamiah, the Presbyterian stronghold on the reservation, and at Lapwai, sixty-five miles to the west, the administrative center of the reservation. At the same time other Nez Perces at Lapwai celebrated the new holiday in more traditional fashion. As noted above, these simultaneous celebrations often led to confrontations between factions within the tribe.

In 1885 the exiled Nez Perces from the war of 1877 arrived home from Indian Territory on July 4 and were welcomed at the Lapwai camp meeting in a restrained but moving ceremony of speeches and prayers, after which for an hour friends filed past to shake the hand of each returning person and to ask after long-lost friends and brothers.[27] Thereafter the Fourth of July was a symbol both of the white Christian nation the missionaries represented and of the return from exile of those who had resisted the white man. Hoping to counteract the tension that continued to exist between the traditional (non-Christian) and the Christian Nez Perces, the agent urged them to join together in 1887 to celebrate the Fourth. This they did, but the Presbyterian Nez Perces and the missionaries complained increasingly of the bad influence of the "heathens." In 1891, Jane Gay encouraged them to urge the agent to forbid the traditional Nez Perces their dress parade, at least in the vicinity of the school. As a result the "heathens" moved their celebration a short distance away, where it was an annual temptation to Presbyterian youths (and missionaries)[28] until after 1897, when the government stopped it altogether.

Jane Gay seems not to have had second thoughts about what to us seems an unfortunate exacerbation of divisions among the Nez Perces. To her it was enough that "Her Majesty" approved.

Jane Gay describes Alice Fletcher in these letters but she tells us very little of what Fletcher is thinking. For Fletcher's version of the events recounted in these letters there are several other sources. Fletcher sent some early reports to *The Morning Star* (which became the *Red Man* in 1888), the newspaper of the Carlisle Indian school; she wrote hundreds of letters to Thomas Jefferson Morgan, the commissioner of Indian Affairs; and she also wrote frequently to Frederic W. Putnam, her scientific mentor.

Fletcher had a close relationship with the Indian industrial school at Carlisle, Pennsylvania, founded by Captain Richard H. Pratt in 1879 as the first nonreservation boarding school exclusively for Indians. She spoke frequently at the school, lobbied in Congress on its behalf, and brought students to it. For a time she was an official "correspondent" of the school paper. In a series of earnest and resolutely optimistic letters in 1887 she explained the implications of the Dawes Act, described her recent experiences in Alaska, and found historical precedent for the Dawes Act in the work of John Eliot, who had founded an Indian town at Natick, Massachusetts, in 1652 and there stressed the learning of trades and individual ownership of homes and gardens.[29]

In 1888, Fletcher wrote to the school from the Winnebago Agency, reporting on the progress of allotment. She started to do the same thing from the Nez Perce Reservation in 1889 but was quickly overwhelmed by the demands of the work.[30] Jane Gay wrote to Captain Pratt instead and suddenly found herself with a new occupation. Pratt liked her wry and funny letter, which he subtitled "A Rich and Racy View of a Trying Situation," and henceforth increasing amounts of space in the *Red Man* were given to letters "from the companion of Miss Fletcher."[31] Most of the letters in the first half of this volume were printed in the *Red Man* between 1889 and 1891.[32]

Meanwhile, Alice Fletcher wrote official letters several times a week to the commissioner of Indian affairs, Thomas J. Morgan, who, with his wife, was a personal friend of hers. Fletcher asked for advice and for orders and decisions on particular points, requested necessary supplies, and sent vouchers and bills. She also gave full descriptions of her difficulties and of the intense resistance to allotment which she encountered. But she did not and in fact felt that she could not waver, because that "would have been unfair to the hundreds of law abiding Indians who had already accepted the law and taken their lands."[33] She had embarked on a program in which she believed, and for her there was no turning back.

To Frederic W. Putnam, Fletcher expressed quite another side of herself, sentiments of which even Jane Gay may not have been fully aware. These concerned the deep ambivalence she felt, not about the allotment program, but about the choice she had made to work for the government and for Indian welfare rather than to continue to do science.

Shortly after she was sent to Idaho in 1889, she wrote to her scientific mentor of her great disappointment at being ordered off on short notice without having a chance to complete the study of Omaha Indian music on which she was working. "I had to go," she wrote, "but it was to give up what I cared most for. I want to honor your friendship and kindness to me, and here I am down in the cañons of the Clearwater, and the rocky steeps that shut me in from all the world, seem like the walls of fate about me. Don't give me up. I will get the work done and before long, I trust."[34] Repeatedly Fletcher referred to her western post as "the wilderness," the biblical place of exile to which she had been consigned. She stole time to finish the music monograph and to work on a paper on the Winnebago alphabet which she wanted to send to the upcoming meeting of the American Association for the Advancement of Science, in part by rising before dawn.[35]

The conflict about her choice of work was settled in theory during the summer of 1890 when Fletcher learned that Mary C. Thaw, the widow of a Pittsburgh railroad and steel magnate, had endowed a lifetime fellowship for her at the Peabody Museum. Henceforth Fletcher did not have to work for the Bureau of Indian Affairs but could devote herself to science. But her satisfaction was deferred because in her words, "honor and justice demand that I finish this reservation."[36] The task took a good part of the next three years, and Fletcher's frustrations grew as the difficulties increased.

Fletcher published very little on the Nez Perces. While on the reservation she was so preoccupied with the immediate problems of allotment that there was little time for disinterested research. Nevertheless, she tried. She took extensive notes on Nez Perce customs and collected material artifacts for the Peabody Museum.[37] She encouraged the missionary Sue L. McBeth to complete the dictionary and grammar of the Nez Perce language on which Miss McBeth had been working with Harry Haynes, a Nez Perce. She also recorded a great deal of information from Jonathan Williams, an elderly man whom Fletcher considered the most reliable authority on Nez Perce history.[38]

Each winter Alice Fletcher and Jane Gay returned to Washington. In 1892 they moved to a small home at 214 First Street, S.E., which Mrs. Thaw helped Fletcher purchase and which they shared with Francis La Flesche, whom Fletcher had adopted informally as her son.

"214," as it was often called, was soon one of the famous places in Washington. Simon Newcomb, the economist and astronomer, and Ainsworth Spofford, President Lincoln's secretary and later Librarian of Congress, were among those who frequented "Miss Fletcher's" drawing room on her day at home. Jane Gay's niece and namesake, Jane Gay Dodge, sometimes poured tea for these occasions and remembered that scientists, artists, handsome congressmen, and representatives from all levels of Washington society were present. She also recalled a Mrs. Lauder, famous actress and "grande dame," who would appear at Miss Fletcher's to play whist with her crony Miss Gay.[39]

In 1894 the Nez Perce allotments were finally finished. With little regret Fletcher put government work behind her and devoted her attention to science. She and Francis La Flesche worked on their long transcription of a Pawnee ceremony, *The Hako*, and on their major study, *The Omaha Tribe* (1911).[40] Fletcher also was active in numerous scientific organizations: vice-president of the American Association for the Advancement of Science, president of the Women's Anthropological Society and of the Anthropological Society of Washington, a founding member of the American Anthropological Association, and president of the American Folklore Society. Meanwhile Jane Gay, the "famous cook and carpenter" who "could do everything better than anybody," kept the household lively.[41]

Fletcher and Gay often went their separate ways in the summer, with Fletcher visiting friends in Europe, California, or Mexico and Jane Gay traveling or visiting family members. In 1906, when she was seventy-six years old, Jane Gay and a niece, Emma Gay, went to England on a journey that was to be the beginning of a new chapter in their lives.

In London the two Misses Gay looked up Dr. Caroline Sturge (1861–1922), a physician and member of a prominent

Quaker family from Bristol and friend of Jane Gay's physician in Washington, Dr. Anne Wilson.[42] Dr. Sturge was examiner in operative midwifery at the Royal Free Hospital Medical School and a practicing midwife in London. To make ends meet, Dr. Sturge had for a time run a boarding house in London, but when Jane Gay met her, she was living alone and was lonely. A warm friendship grew between the two women, and in 1907 Jane Gay decided to make her home in England with Dr. Sturge, a woman who valued her friends above all else. They lived in London until 1909, when "the fog and darkness of a London winter" began to tell on Jane Gay's health.[43] Then Dr. Sturge used an inheritance she had received to retire from her midwifery practice and move to the country, to Congresbury, a village near Bristol, with Jane Gay and Emma Gay. There Jane Gay tended a large flower garden, and they welcomed many visitors, including Alice Fletcher. During World War I, when the women had difficulty getting household help, Dr. Sturge built a smaller cottage at Winscombe, which they named "Kamiah" for the peaceful place in Idaho that Jane Gay had loved. Jane Gay died at Kamiah in 1919. Alice Fletcher continued to live with Francis La Flesche at "214" until her death in 1923.

In 1895, Jane Gay and Emma Gay began to put together the letters and photographs from Idaho into a book which they titled *Choup-nit-ki* (With the Nez Perces). Emma Gay did pen and ink drawings for the two volumes and bound them herself in London in 1909. These leather-bound volumes, locked in their specially made wooden boxes, were donated to Radcliffe College by Jane Gay Dodge in 1951. There they are now part of the manuscript collections of the Schlesinger Library.

The letters are reprinted here substantially as they appear in the original two volumes, although we have shortened them by approximately one-fourth, omitting repetitious and overlong descriptive passages. The original paragraphing has been retained, but obvious misspellings have been corrected, and the punctuation has in a few cases been altered slightly for easier reading. Ellipses (. . .) indicate editorial deletions, but asterisks (* * *) are Jane Gay's and indicate major breaks in the original text (Gay often wrote one letter over several days or from more than one location). Notes have been supplied to identify people, places, and events mentioned in the text.

The original volumes contained 191 photographs. Thirty-eight have been reproduced here, along with two others from the Jane Gay Collection of the Idaho State Historical Society that were not included in the hand-bound books. (For a full description of the Jane Gay holdings in the Idaho State Historical Society, see *Jane Gay Photograph Collection Catalog*, compiled by Lilian W. Dawson, with an introduction by Alan G. Marshall [Boise: Idaho State Historical Society, 1980].) The photograph captions in quotation marks are Jane Gay's; other information about the photographs, much of it supplied by the Idaho State Historical Society, has been added by the editors.

Choup-nit-ki
With the Nez Perces
by E. Jane Gay

Prefatory Note

To those not conversant with Government legislation in regard to the aborigines of our country, it may be well to say that after narrowing the tribal lands to the extreme limit of prudence, and it began to look as if the ever encroaching white man would "take" all that was then left, Congress, on February 8th, 1887, passed the Land in Severalty Act, commonly called the Dawes Bill.

This Bill gave to each Indian an allotment of his tribal land and secured it to him by trust patent, to be superseded after twenty-five years by fee simple patent.

Special Agents were appointed by the President to apportion these lands, and "Her Majesty," Alice C. Fletcher, was among the first to be sent to the field in that capacity, having already allotted the Omaha tribe under a special Act.

Setting aside, in the meantime, her ethnological pursuits, she allotted the Winnebago tribe and then went to the Nez Perces and it was from the Nez Perce reservation in the then Territory of Idaho, that these letters were written by an unofficial member of her party.

They were addressed to personal friends from whom they have been gathered by the compiler.

Few liberties have been taken with the text; only a little blurring of personal identity, and necessary omissions of private mention: the foundation facts have not been disturbed.

G.

Washington, D.C.   August, 1895

Letter One

LEWISTON, IDAHO
May 30th, 1889

I hardly dare hope that this letter will come within the scope of my promise "to write by the way," for we are actually over the Rockies. In fact, we have arrived, and are pausing here, at the last Post Office station, to take a few more free breaths, before we cut our communications and plunge into the unknown. After we had left Chicago, I began to feel as if I had already a new lease of life in this open, free land of breath and sun. It is superb, wonderful, and makes one wish he could begin all over again and work out a new term of existence, wider from the very start. I have a nipped-in-the-bud feeling when I see what advantages they have who have been born into a large place. Why! we did not know that we could breathe deeper, or think faster, until we began to spin along over the green illimitable prairies.

And then we passed the Yellowstone Park and entered the Gallatin Valley, enclosed by ranges of snow-capped hills, and here, among herds of cattle galloping towards us, we see our first cowboy. And by-and-by we stop at Helena and take on two Jumbo engines and begin our ascent of the Rockies. We wind up, turning upon our track again and again, until at last, we reach the top and pass through a tunnel and come out the other side, where the streams flow the other way. The two big engines hold back and we have the air brake on and we bump along for twenty-four hours before we reach the lake Pend Oreille, which you must make a pilgrimage to see. Our train winds about the lake for an hour before it can make up its mind to go on and everybody is sorry when the echo of the good-bye whistle dies out over the placid surface of the water and we are on the straight line again. We came down from Spokane Falls on a spur of the Northern Pacific Railroad and had the good fortune to reach Uniontown after dark.

Our Photographer, who is of Scottish descent, turns out to be the most philosophic, if not the most original, member of our party. When, in the morning sun, the bald grime of our surroundings was vividly revealed, it was the Photographer who was the least staggered of us all. Now, Uniontown does not materially differ from the usual transitory settlement at the movable terminus of a western railroad. One straight street, unpaved and unclean, over which cattle roam as "commoners," a blacksmith's shop at one end, the "hotel" at the other, and between, a miscellaneous store, a good many evil-smelling saloons and a house or two set directly on the street, where people who have to stay eat and sleep. It is but a type of many such places where human beings actually do live; where men die and children are born,—only we had stepped out of a palace car into it, with the majesty and beauty of uncontaminated nature still unfaded from our mental retina, and none of us save the Photographer was disposed to speculate or theorize.

He said, with the air of a connoisseur, as we stood upon the rough board piazza of our hotel, watching two pigs quarrel over the possession of a refuse heap and trying to guess the number of nationalities represented in a group of men who were also interested in the exciting spectacle,—he said that America was a country of immense possibilities and that its digestive forces were marvellous. We remembered this remark afterward while struggling with our breakfast, and we ate our boiled eggs in thankfulness with an unspoken blessing on the benign pullet of the Great West.

A drive of two hours, behind a team of four stout half-breed horses, brought us and our trunks down to Lewiston. The way lay along ranches where herds of cattle and droves of horses ("bunches," in Idaho parlance,) were grazing on the new spring grass, the little colts with their dams and the calves frisking and kicking up their heels at our approach.

Troops of gray squirrels ran across the road and in some places the grass appeared alive with them. Once, their dead bodies lay thickly strewn along the edge of the way, poisoned by some ranchman as intolerable pests.

The last five miles of our journey was a sheer zig-zag fall of two thousand feet down to the Snake River, at the junction of which with the Clearwater River lies the queer little sunburnt town of Lewiston reminding one of the hamlets on the moraines in Norway. . . . But this Idaho road is not picturesque like the government roads of Norway. It is simply something to be gotten over as quickly as possible, as our driver seemed fully to realize.

We saw real Robin Red-breasts as we dashed along at a breakneck speed and they sang as if they had never been molested by the pugnacious sparrow. The bee martins and the meadowlarks sat upon the upper wire of the fences and trilled out a welcome until our spirits rose with the melody as we and our trunks tumbled to the bottom and we crossed the ferry and landed at our "Hotel," ready to see all things in the roseate hue of hope.

The archaeological member of our party has already ascertained that this hotel was set up in the early mining days, in a tent, upon this very spot, by a Frenchwoman of energy and respectability.[1] The tent has developed by slow degrees into a very substantial, rather rambling, frame house, boarded within and without with the pine wood of the country, and the people are still French, with the one exception of the porter, a "sticket" Scotchman, who lost his grip in California years ago, and has been dazed ever since. He replies to our questions, as Don Quixote might have done, with deferential stateliness. I asked him if a letter put in the box last night had gone in this morning's mail? He said, "Peradventure it might"; he would do himself the pleasure to ascertain definitely in a brief period of time.

Our landlady is a brisk, kindly little body and the waiters are gray-haired men who have also the look of having been stranded upon the shore of ill luck. They speak English with a French accent and all manifest a fatherly interest in our little company. And so we take our ease at our Inn and sip our coffee, while our elderly waiter caps our strawberries and our roving eyes catch, through the window opposite, the gleam of long rows of snow-white linen, out to dry, and we know that the Chinaman is also here.

Our arrival was noticed in the newspaper of the place and we have been called upon by several of the prominent people. We are told that there is confusion at the Agency, owing to a change of Agents, and that internecine war is raging among the officials. Three of them are on trial here in the county court for assault with intent to kill and for false imprisonment of each other. They all go armed and even the women of their families are accused of fighting with fists.

Each of the contending parties has called upon the Allotting Agent, to warn her against all the rest, and the three Special Agents, sent from Washington to quell the Indian official "rising," have also been to enlighten her upon the situation. None of them can give her any idea as to where, how, and when to begin her especial work, but all agree that it is going to be a difficult task.

They report that the Indians are "disturbed," which does not surprise us, and that there are many signs of hostility on their part which we would do well to heed. On inquiring the causes of this hostility, we are told that a former Agent who is peculiarly obnoxious to the tribe is being pressed upon the Government for a reappointment, which they are determined to resist.[2] We are also advised, considering the unquiet condition of the Reservation, to ask for the presence of a company of United States soldiers from Walla Walla.

The Allotting Agent makes no response to this advice, but the cook anxiously asks if there is any danger of the troops coming *before* they are called for?

The object of the Nez Perce hostility has also called to see us and has been prolific of his offers of friendly assistance, even inviting us to make his house our headquarters when he shall be installed as Agent.

* * *

The Allotting Agent hired a pair of horses yesterday and has gone to reconnoitre, leaving us in charge of the baggage. The Cook has visited the several stores of the town and has found a sheet iron camp stove and an oil lamp and has invested in a farina kettle. Everybody tells us that the country is lovely, the climate fine, the soil the best in the world and Chinamen do all the work! All the elements, you see, of a paradise. We are sensible of the Chinamen, for Ah Sin has been in and saturated my bedstead, floor and walls, with a gallon canful of kerosene oil, and the house is being cleaned in the same way from the centre to the circumference. The Photographer, who has been picking up scraps of information from the people, says we have indeed reached a Land of Goshen. "Everything from wheat to peanuts will grow here. Potatoes yield an immense crop! Strawberries are about gone for the season, so are cherries, but apricots, nectarines and peaches are coming on. It is a little too cold in the winter for oranges, ice forming sometimes in the lowlands and snow falling on the mountains, but every kind of vegetable is cultivated and everything is *so* cheap! Idaho is the garden spot of the earth!" While we were listening, entranced, to this recital, a dust storm broke upon the town and for an hour we gasped and struggled to breathe the clouds of alkaline dust which surged up against our hotel and penetrated to our room.

"Do you have much rain?" I asked the landlady, after the storm had subsided and only occasionally a whirlwind bore past great columns of sand.

"Rain!" said she, "there's no rain in this country from June to October, and often not for six months at a time.

* * *

The Allotting Agent has returned and says we are to go upon the Reservation tomorrow. She has had a conversation through the telephone with a surveyor, a Mr. Briggs, whom she has engaged to meet us at Lapwai. She does not say much about the situation and, in answer to the Cook's anxious questioning, she bids us not to "cross a bridge before we come to it," whatever that may mean. The Cook mutters that it is very well for a sentiment; for her part, she wants to know what the bridge is made of *before* she puts her foot on it.

* * *

I have retained this letter to give you our first impressions of what is to be our abiding place and workshop for many months to come.

Our ride from Lewiston was a new sensation. First, we climbed up out of the town, making the two thousand feet of circuitous ascent in a painfully cautious manner, jumping out to walk up the steepest hills and arriving at the top in a breathless, spent condition, where we halted to rest the horses. Then we bowled along over the road, which is little more than a trail, kicking up clouds of dust, which, the wind being at our back, we could not run away from and often could not see through. Some ten miles of this comparatively level trail brought us to the edge of a cañon down which we plunged, over rocks and through gullies, swaying from side to side and bumping up and down, slipping and sliding and pitching headforemost, until, when we came out upon the valley of Lapwai, we had reached the utmost limit of our endurance. We were told for our comfort that the road was not quite as good as usual, "a water-spout having broken in it a little while ago." In fact, our driver said, it was "most worn out." It had lasted ever since the time when Lapwai was a garrisoned fort, having been originally made by the soldiers, but, worn out as it was, via Soldier's Cañon was still the best route to the Reservation.

Lapwai valley lies chiefly on the western side of Lapwai Creek, which runs between two ranges of foot hills and is very narrow in spots, broadening out again so as to make space for gardens and little homes for the Indians. The hills are covered in early spring by the native grasses, which do not make a turf, but grow in bunches, furnishing a very nutritious food for cattle. A little later in the season the hills are bare and brown and show plainly the terraces made by the feet of cattle as they roam along the sides, grubbing the very roots of the dried grass. Along the edges of the creek there is a scanty growth of thorn bushes and a few stunted trees. . . . Three miles to the north, down the valley where the creek runs into the Clearwater river, is the Agency site, where the local Agent and his Cabinet live, the farmer, and the carpenter and the doctor.

At the time of our arrival, there being an interregnum, one Agent having been removed and his successor not yet installed, a special Agent was in charge of the Reservation and he had made his headquarters at Lapwai in one of the buildings under the western hills of the valley. He has given us an unstinted welcome, a gracious hospitality grateful to tired wayfarers. . . .

* * *

We have bought cotton cloth for a tent and are preparing for our first campaign. Special Agent Wilton and his daughter are giving us valuable aid and advice the tone of which, the Cook says, is encouraging rather than congratulatory. I dare say he knows what we need at the outset of our undertaking. Congratulations may be in order at the finish. The Surveyor has come to arrange with the Allotting Agent how the campaign shall begin. Mr. Briggs is a Vermonter by birth, who has been west long enough to thoroughly know the country. He is a big, broad-shouldered man, with a face that wins your confidence at once. He blushed and seemed confused, when introduced to the Allotting Agent, and was not at ease until he had explained that, having accepted Her Majesty's proposal by telephone, he was not aware that he had made an engagement with a lady. Then after a hearty laugh, he entered upon a discussion of the work with such a comprehensive knowledge of its details that one great cause of anxiety has been removed. He knows the lay of the land and will be of immense help in the proper placing of the Indians.

Already we have been called upon by a delegation of Cattlemen, who desire to know what the Allotting Agent proposes to do about their "rights" upon the Reservation. They seem to be utterly ignorant of the intent of the Severalty Act. I am afraid they take it to be a skilful contrivance to dispossess the aborigines and facilitate the opening up of their lands to squatter sovereignty.

Her Majesty read her instructions to the delegation and explained that it was her sworn duty to place the Indians upon their best lands and in the localities where they would most rapidly become self-supporting and valuable citizens, not so to dispose of them that they must be paupers and a charge upon the white population of the territory. The men are evidently non-plussed, for, as they mounted their horses the Photographer heard one mutter, "Why in thunder did the Government send a woman to do this work? We could have got a holt on a man." They "sound" the Surveyor before they ride away and he tells them he does not as yet know anything as to their prospects, but he rather thinks "from the looks of the Allotting Agent's eye, that everything will have to be done on the square." The introduction of the square idea has a depressing effect, for hitherto they have worked only in rings, but I dare say they really have no faith in anybody being able to square their circle.

Do not imagine that these cattlemen are in the least like your interesting cowboys. There is nothing romantic about them. For the greater part, they are farmers in the neighborhood who raise crops on their own land and turn out their cattle to overrun the Reservation. We are told that there are approximately ten thousand head now eating the grass of the Indians, who are also cattlemen in their own right, and have none too much pasturage for their own herds. . . .

Letter Two

Lapwai,
June 8th, 1889

At last our tent is finished, James the interpreter, having obligingly run up its final seam.[3]

Although it has taken the combined energies of our entire community to build it, Special Agent Wilton has really been the Alpha and Omega of that tent. He it was who cut the canvas, after his own specially invented device, and it was he who put on the final touch by stencilling Her Majesty's name above the top of the door flap; and then we all went out on the campus and pitched the tent and crawled in and out, and out and in, through the little strip of door until our backs were in danger of contracting a permanent stoop, so delighted were we with the new experience of making ourselves small enough to fit our environment.

Our tent is of the truncated cone shape and warranted to keep us dry if it should, by any unforeseen possibility, rain while we are in the field. James says it is also "snake proof, but no good to keep out squirrels." Our camp bedstead is a model of ingenuity.

It shuts up for transportation, but can be made a table, lounge or bed at will; our tent stove can be flattened out like a sheet of pasteboard and stowed under the camp chest, its pipe tied under the wagon with the tent pole, which is in four pieces and put together like a patent fish rod and is to have, fastened at the top, a U.S. flag.

When we arrived here, we found a Chinaman on duty, and until we could put our own affairs in good working order, we joined his "Mess." . . . Gooey is a good fellow, good from some innate principle of his own, which works independently of his surroundings. He toils all the day and half the night; he does everything there is to be done in the quarters, for we soon discovered that if we tried to help in any way we should lose his respect. He does everything by halves but everything by wholesale; in his eye, our frugal little party is magnified into a voracious regiment and provided for accordingly and no amount of calm reason or indignant expostulation has any effect upon the preconceived notions of the Chinaman as to what should constitute a "Melican" bill of fare. The Cook has had the providing for the family laid upon her and has borne the responsibility of her position uncomplainingly, but it is telling upon her amiability.

Once a week, in the early morning, she crawls up out of Soldier's Cañon and drives to Lewiston through opaque clouds of alkaline dust, in search of fruit and vegetables and beef; for some of us are vegetarians and some are carnivora.

For so small a company, our dispositions and tastes are very diverse. She returns at nightfall, bruised with the jolting over stones, her lungs full of the pulverized pumice soil, and her wagon packed with a week's supply of the best the market affords. To accomplish this she has made a journey of twenty-four miles, ransacked the town and exploited the one market garden in the vicinity. But her labors have just begun. Now she enters upon a series of complicated subterfuges and ingenious strategems to keep Gooey from cooking everything she has brought, all at once, the first day. It is amusing to the rest of us to watch the drama, but it is demoralizing to the Cook; and as to Gooey, if he understands her machinations, he gives no sign. His imperturbable smile never relaxes but, be the Cook for one moment off guard, he goes in and wins and then we have warmed up dinners for the rest of the week.

We put up with these little idiosyncrasies which are dwarfed in the light of the Chinaman's great excellencies, for he is the personification of cleanliness and, at the present moment, I can imagine no superior virtue. He is never visible except when clothed in spotless white linen, unsullied white stockings and slippers, and with his long black queue neatly wound about his shining head. The Cook, who rises long before it is day, always finds Gooey at work and the Photographer declares that he irons his white linen blouse at four o'clock in the morning.

Faithful old Gooey! we would trust him with all we possess,—except our digestive powers.

He is fond of children and the small Nez Perces lie in wait for him on the path to the trader's store, where candy and peanuts slip into their little hands and the pennies out of Gooey's pockets. He is also fond of his "Mudder" and talks incoherently of going back to China to see her, when he draws his pay from the Indian Bureau for his services as cook to the Government School in the last administration. We think Gooey will see his Mudder in another country than China before the tangle of red tape, which has become cocooned about his claim, can be unraveled. Meanwhile, he plods on in unstinted industry, a reproach and an aggravation to some of us who are trying to persuade ourselves that we are doing our whole duty in our own sphere, yet conscious of shortcomings in the light of the Chinaman's example.

I see him at this moment, his day's work done, at twilight, mounted on his wild Indian pony, without saddle or bridle, a rope halter connecting him with the animal; his loose blouse puffed out in the breeze, his long queue flapping up and down with the movement of his horse and the children hallowing and throwing up their caps and turning somersaults in the grass as is their wont when Gooey rides. It is his one recreation and we, who have watched the performance, wonder wherein his enjoyment lies. Her Majesty suggests that there is rest in change of work; the Photographer thinks that the recreation idea must largely be promoted by a change of scene and the Cook expresses the opinion that the chief ingredient in Gooey's pleasure is "the ability to make something go."

He comes back at a gallop, his small slippered feet dug into the sides of his pony, his arms akimbo, his raiment bulging in the disturbed atmosphere, his hatless head catching and reflecting the glow of the aftermath, and his queue still keeping time to the rhythm of his beast.

* * *

The Sunday after our arrival on the Reservation we attended church at the Agency and heard a native preacher expound Christianity. We did not understand one word of the vernacular, but it was interesting to see the dark faces lighted up with a glow of some sort of inspiration; it was pleasant to think that the Indian was able to leave his world of perplexities outside the walls of the little church and to relax his habitual scowl of bewilderment in the contemplation of one simple idea.

We noticed a bright-eyed, calm-faced white woman moving among them as one who was about her Father's business. She seemed the guiding spirit of the service, which moved on in consonance with the dignity and sweetness of her countenance. After the benediction, she introduced herself to us as the missionary, Miss Kate McBeth, and it was interesting to note her scrutiny of us, the guarded expression of her eyes, her cautious speech, the evident search for indications of our disposition towards her Indians. It spoke volumes of her compressed life under the bonds of her position. By and by she seemed to have concluded to trust us and with a smile gave us welcome to her little home. She has temporary quarters in an old warehouse, there by sufferance of the late Agent, but it is already rumored that she will soon be requested to move out of that. A potato shed at Lapwai, which the school superintendent may allow her to occupy, is the only home open to her.

She is cheerful at the prospect. "It will be more comfortable than a tent," she said.

"And," added the Photographer, "all gates to Heaven are not golden."

* * *

Briggs tells us that the white people generally are greatly excited over the "opening of the Reservation," as they call it. The newspapers are swelling the excitement with fabulous accounts of the riches "locked up" in the Indian land, and men are actually, at this early date, flocking into the nearby towns, so as to be ready to "go in" when the rush comes. But the people who show the most interest in us are the cattlemen of the vicinity.

A good many of them have come in person to announce their wishes and to "sound" the Special Agent as to her purpose. What they want to know is: Are they to be defrauded of their rights to free grazing on the Reservation; is the cutting up of the Indian's land into homes for the people to cut also into the ranges of these cattlemen, or will Her Majesty kindly locate the Nez Perces down in the cañons where they belong? They are embarrassed, these "bold highwaymen," as the Cook calls them, not knowing how to "approach" a lady.

It is a study to watch Her Majesty as she listens so respectfully to their intimations; the way she persistently misunderstands them, taking it for granted that they desire above all things the welfare of the Indians; the obtuseness of her to the hints of what might be "to her interest" which are quietly let fall, and are as innocuous as rain drops upon a placid lake. The men hang about day after day, with profuse expectoration, and finally go away, Her Majesty bidding them a cheerful adieu with an encouraging word about the better times coming, when there will be a reign of law and order in the country, which does not always call up a pleasing prospect in the mind of the cattlemen. One of them lost his self-control in the enforced contemplation of such an innovation.

"Law!" said he, with what the Cook calls "border emphasis," "Law! ——— it; what do we want with law? We don't want no law. Never had no law; we've got along so far taking care of ourselves; we done as we wanted to and ain't got no use for law in this country."

* * *

I suppose I am expected to tell you something about our special work; what progress we are making in the allotting of the Indian's land.

We started from Washington with instructions which read easy. "Anybody can allot Indians," said a callow clerk to me one day.

I did not argue with him. I only said, "I suppose you first catch your Indians." He stared at me and I saw that he expected them to be found, all in a row at the Agency, waiting in immovable patience to be labelled in consecutive order and numbered upon the nicely photographed plates furnished by the department. He was dumb when I spoke of "catching" his Indians.

We have now been on the Reservation long enough to have gained an inside view of the peculiar workings of the Agency System, and have learned, as well, the difficulties in the way of our just dealing with the Indians in the matter of their allotments.

We were told that the Nez Perce tribe numbered from eight hundred to two thousand souls and we were to convince them, man, woman and child, of the desirableness of breaking their tribal relations, giving up their tribal rights under U.S. treaty, for American citizenship and a very moderately sized farm cut out of their tribal inheritance.

There might be a little time consumed in this simple preliminary work, but that accomplished, things would move quickly.

"It is not going to be a long job," said the callow clerk, "The Indians are all ready for allotment."

A good many other people said pretty much the same to us. Some, who did not live in Washington, seemed to believe that the wards of the Nation under its paternal care had been led quite out of barbarism up to the very gate of citizenship, that we had but to open the gate and they would tumble over each other in their haste to come in.

Well, my dear J., here we are and it is lonesome, it is queer, and the longer we stay the queerer it grows. Our energies are worn out in trying to get a start. There is no fulcrum whereon to rest a lever, no reliable data to be found. We are in an irresponsible world, where everything hangs in the air—and the air is full of ominous rumors.

It is a significant fact that we have had to go off the Reservation to find the first man who knows anything about the Nez Perce tribe. He is a little wiry Scotchman "of meek demeanor and strong sense," who served in the Joseph war, fought the Indians with all his might, became interested in them, and ended by becoming their fast friend. We found him in Lewiston, working for the most important merchant of the place.

"Yes," said he, "I know the Nez Perces and they know me." He expressed a grave concern for the condition of things on the Reservation, saying that "the Nez Perces are men and not to be trifled with, but easily managed by fair play. I am as fond of them as of my own children."

Mr. McConville offered every assistance in his power to give Her Majesty.[4] He advised me to have great patience as it would take time to win the confidence of the Indians, without which the proper accomplishment of her work would be impossible.

"And the soldiers might have to be sent for," suggested the Cook. "God forbid," said the Scotchman, himself an old soldier.

* * *

Mr. Briggs has been reconnoitering along the bounds of the Reservation. He says it is going to be a "jolly bit of work" to fix the treaty line as he is required to do for the allotment. He finds that the original survey does not conform to the terms of the treaty and that subsequent surveys have been run, each new one inside the last, and that there are farms and houses all along the border upon the Indians' land. The Nez Perces know this and you may imagine how our movements will be watched; with suspicion by the Indians and with greedy eyes by the white people.

Her Majesty has been searching among the wreck of the interregnum for a census roll. James says that if there were a census roll, it would be of no use in the allotment because the common agency practice of giving any name you please to an Indian which he will not answer to, is confusing. But the search for the census roll is as nothing compared with the search for the Indian himself. The race disappeared from the agency horizon before our arrival,—not altogether though. The Indian policemen loiter about the agency, waiting for the new master, whoever he may be. It is their duty to fetch and carry for him so long as they wear the uniform. Now and then a judge of the Indian Court of Offences passes through the valley,[5] mostly at a gallop, and on Sundays there is no lack of a congregation in the little Lapwai church. There is, however, no lingering after service. As soon as the benediction is pronounced, there is a hurried mounting of ponies and a swift disappearance over the hills. The Nez Perces will not come to us; it is clear that we must go to them.

We ask the Special Agent in temporary charge, "Where are the Indians?"

He is a stranger to the place, but he says, "Indians? oh, they're all about."

Now the Reservation comprises nearly 800,000 acres; is crossed and recrossed by cañons, cut into by gulches, broken by hills and buttes and rocky wastes and traversed by a confusing network of cattle and pony trails.[6] Hunting a needle in a haymow may be successful in time. You can remove straw after straw and if the needle be in the stack, it will appear in the end if only you have sharp enough eyes, but we climb over weary miles of almost impassable country, scrambling over sharp trap rock, broken like the refuse from a quarry, and we do not come upon an Indian. He may have a local habitation and a name, but the man himself is peripatetic. You may see his cabin perched far up on a bench or bluff, but two sticks leaning against the door will tell you that the owner is not at home, and far down below at the bottom of the gulch, lies his little garden patch, dried up and deserted, the spring which had fed it having sacrificed its last drop to worship of the Sun.

We make this sort of reconnoissance three or four times, penetrating farther and farther into the interior, by aid of the government team furnished by courtesy of the interregnum Agent, but to no purpose; and then we decide that Mahomet cannot go to the Mountain any more.

In the hope that something might come of it, Her Majesty asks the friendly Agent to issue a call for the Indians to meet in council and he sends out a native policeman on a pony, and, while awaiting the result, we inquire about the available means of transportation. If the Government furnished balloons, we would feel encouraged as we contemplate the other side of yawning abysses, and the towering mountains beyond. If it permitted pontoons, we might hope to triumph over the treacherous fords of unreliable mountain streams which must be crossed, but we lie awake at night trying to solve the problem. We are allowed to have a pair of horses and a wagon, which, to be strong enough, will weigh several hundred pounds, and into which must be packed our entire camp equipage, food supplies and forage for several weeks' consumption. Besides, *we* are not imponderable bodies. Her Majesty, however, spiritually minded, is substantially materialized, and no one has ever dared attribute to cook, photographer, and friend anything more ethereal than a little irresponsible lightheadedness. And there is James, our driver and interpreter; we have to carry his heavy responsibilities. How are we to make a solvable equation of these factors?

We rise in the morning, unrefreshed, and set out upon the search for that pivotal pair of horses. First, we look over the resources of the Agency. There are several animals in the stables and we try them all. One backs when going up hill, another runs away when going down. Two are work horses, used in plowing and hauling, one is a vicious stallion, one is totally blind; one is lame in the right shoulder and all look moth eaten and fly blown. In a lean-to against the south side of the stable, we find a Webster wagon, a buckboard and an ambulance, all of which had been preempted by the chickens as roosting places and none of which seem adapted to our purpose.

We finally inquire of the Agency farmer if there is not a man in the vicinity who has horses to sell, and for answer, the next morning that man arrives with "the only team to be had short of seventy miles. It is a half-breed team, good and spry; just what you want," says the man.

We inquire the price and are told that "nothing short of four hundred dollars will buy that team." We murmur something about the price being "steep" but we think of the steepness of the trails and are conscious of bondage; we have no choice either as to hills or horses. But the matter must be laid before the Department three thousand miles away, and while waiting its action, the Special Agent hears of a team which had been bought for the use of a Government commission, now out of service, said team having been left on a neighboring Reservation, and she asks for a transfer of the animals to her.

The request is granted by telegraph and the driver is sent for the beasts at the risk of his life, for the mercury stands at 110° and the road to Umatilla is over an arid plain and through a doubly heated cañon. But the horses arrive at the end of a week and we all go out to meet them.

They stop in the middle of the road and look at us inquiringly. James said they were "kind" and they did look as if they would not hurt a fly. Somehow we had a misgiving as we stood before those horses. The expression of their harness, which was matchless in its way, may have prejudiced us. The off horse, Dick, wore a pair of blinders oval in outline, flat, and lying close upon his eyeballs, while those of Jimmy, his mate, were square, concave, and protruding at an angle of forty-five degrees from the side of his head. The tugs were spliced roughly in several places; there was no mystery about the collars, their internal construction being clearly indicated on the outside, and the headstalls were held in place by bits of many-colored twine. The wagon harmonized perfectly with the harness. James said that the horses had been foundered, when we called his attention to their hoofs and the Surveyor said they needed shoeing; the Cook suggested a soaking, in the wild hope of softening the iron frogs; the Photographer said that they ought to rest before we tried any experiments upon them;—so they were led away to be hobbled and turned loose to do as they pleased.

"They know best what is good for them," said the Photographer, but in half an hour, the Cook (triumphantly) reported that they were standing in Lapwai Creek.

Now the Surveyor and Her Majesty hold a private consultation, the outcome of which is that Briggs shall patch up the wagon and Her Majesty have the harness repaired and pay for it out of her own pocket; "it was such a trifling expense." But it did not prove to be such a small affair, for the first time the harness was used it broke in a new place and kept on doing that sort of thing until we all agreed with the Cook who "despised makeshifts that put one's life in peril" and Her Majesty was compelled to make an exigency purchase of new harness.

And now we are astonished at the improvement in our two horses. They hold their heads erect in evident pride; they step off gaily; "the consciousness of being well dressed," says the Cook, "is a stimulant to good behavior."

Today is Saturday. On Monday we expect to meet the Indians in council in response to the call of the Agent. After that is over, I may have some progress to record. Till then, Au revoir.

Letter Three

Lapwai,
June 29th, 1889

When I last wrote, we were expecting the Indians to meet us in council the coming Monday. We were told that the prospect of a council always "brought them in," but we had so universally found them out on our various expeditions to their nominal homes and had met with so slight a trace of human occupancy anywhere, that but for the one fact of having seen a church full at the Agency on Sundays, we might have come to the conclusion that the Nez Perce tribe was a myth. There are so many things in the conduct of Indian affairs that have nothing more tangible than a name to live; so many opinions concerning the red man not warranted by facts; so many orchid ideas growing in the air; so many parasitical beliefs hanging on to inherited prejudices, that it would not have greatly surprised us if, on going over to that council room, we should have found it filled with nothing more substantial than U.S. Indian treaties.

But the Nez Perces were there, a handful of them: enough to fill the small room and overflow about the doorway.

It does not seem as if there could be anything in that room to impress very deeply an allotting agent. . . . There is tangible silence within; dark forms are ranged against the walls, some on wooden benches, others standing, and some prone upon the floor. The attitude of all is simply that of waiting—waiting to know what is wanted of them.

You catch no inspiration from their faces as you are introduced by the agent in charge, but you make a little speech as graciously as you are able. There is no halfway meeting of your overtures; only the silence which can be felt.

You read the Severalty Act and explain its provisions.

22

You think you make it plain but the rows of old red sandstone sphinxes make no sign. Their eyes are fixed in stony dumbness. They never heard of the "Dawes' Bill"; they cannot take it in.

Imagine your self, some bright May morning, sitting out upon the horse block in your back yard, waiting for breakfast in that calm state of mind induced by early rising and the prospect of a savory meal. . . . Before you lie broad acres, your own well tilled fields, that were your fathers' before you. They have been in the family for many generations; so long that it has never come into your mind that they could ever be any where else. In retrospect you behold the bent forms of your aged grandparents, standing amid the heavy topped wheat, ripened like themselves; and glancing down the future, you see the children of your boy Tom playing out there upon that sunny knoll among the buttercups and daisies, when you are awakened by the slam of the front gate and the lightning-rod man or a book agent comes round the house and tells you that the Empress of all the Indies, or some other potentate with whom you have treaty relations, has sent him to divide your lands according to act of Parliament, in the year of our Lord, February 8th, 1887.

You stare wildly while the lightning-rod man proceeds to explain, that, as head of the family, you are to have 160 acres of your own land; your boy Tom, being over eighteen, will have 80 acres; and the little girl, the pet, the black-eyed darling, she will have 40 acres.

Mechanically you repeat, "160, 80, 40,—280 acres." That is just the size of your meadow where the cows and horses pasture; but what of the rest?

The lightning-rod man goes on: "The remainder of your land will stay just as it is, *unless you want to sell it.*" Ah! It looks queer, does it?

Little by little you begin to think. . . . Your suspicions are aroused and—you look exactly as those North Americans looked in that Council room.

But now, as Allotting Agent, you stand before them, and, with reddened checks and stammering tongue you try to impress them with the advantages of the proposed arrangement. You had prearranged your arguments and expected to convince this docile people as easily as you had convinced yourself, but somehow you weaken. Your arguments give way before the logic of voiceless helplessness. . . .

Your arteries throb so loudly in the silence that you can think of nothing to say. You ask the Interpreter to tell the Indians that you will be glad to answer any questions, and you sit down. Your cravat is tight and you loosen it. There is a stricture about the cardiac region. You unbutton your coat and look along the line of dark faces. They do not light up as they meet your gaze and it is your own eyes that first seek the ground. But at last an old man rises, with a dignity which renders invisible his poor garments and his low estate and makes you do him reverence.

"How is it," he says, "that we have not been consulted about this matter? Who made this law? We do not understand what you say. This is our land by long possession and by treaty. We are content to be as we are." And a groan of assent runs along the dark line of Sphinxes as the old man draws his blanket about him, as if forevermore to shut out the subject.

The action rouses you and you gather your forces, while the next man in less quiet tones asks if you are not "afraid to come among them on such an errand"! "Our people are scattered," says another. "We must come together and decide whether we will have this law."

You tell them that there is nothing for them to decide; they have no choice. The law must be obeyed, but you will wait until they can understand better all about it. And then, with rare discretion, the ad interim Agent adjourns the council.

As the people disperse amid low mutterings in cheerless tones, you clearly realize that you have not caught your Indian.

You shake hands with one or two as they pass out, but for the most part they avoid you. A few linger and you talk a little. You do not say "I am your friend." That phrase means nothing now to the Indian. You tell them that by and by, when you know each other better, perhaps you may trust each other. And they do not dispute you; it looks reasonable.

At any rate, it postpones the issue and the Indian likes that. He cannot be hurried and you know better than to try to hurry him. He goes home to think over this allotment business or to forget all about it, according to the manner of man he is, but the Special Agent takes the outcome of this her first Council very much to heart. It does not seem to have altered any thing; she is just where she was before. But, while the Cook lays violent hands upon her inclination to resist the patient endurance of inaction, and the Photographer gracefully accepts his laissez-faire role, and the unfeeling Surveyor, who is not new to Reservation experiences, jokes incoherently, as it seems to us, about "tenderfeet" and "eye openers" the Allotting Agent betrays no waver of discouragement at the forbidding aspect of the situation. She studies the topography of the country with Mr. Briggs and opens up a peripatetic school of instruction to inform the "actual settler," who is in Egyptian darkness as to the provisions of the Severalty Act. She loses no opportunity of getting the Indians together in little groups for informal councils, she talks and reasons in the hope of making ever so slight an impression to work out from. . . .

At present, some hidden influence obstructs all her plans. Her employees slip away, one by one, and the Surveyor's chainmen disappear between nightfall and sunrise. Our Interpreter grows haggard and nervous and objects on various pretexts to driving Her Majesty any distance from Lapwai and finally he confesses that his life has been threatened if he continues in her service. We learn also from outside sources that the situation is grave.

You will have gathered from my letters that the Government is forcing upon the tribe as Agent a man they will not accept. They have quietly protested in three petitions, simply asking that, of all men in the country, this one only may not be sent to oppress them in the future as he has done in the past. He was Agent formerly for four years and has spent four other years on the Reservation as Agency Clerk.

The three petitions failed to receive attention and the man has been appointed. When the tidings reached the Indians, "runners" rode all night to summon the tribe to a secret

Council where money was raised and a messenger dispatched to Washington to plead their cause. He has been gone twelve days; whether the tribe has received any word from him, or are carrying out a plan formed before his departure cannot be known, but the Indians have disappeared from their usual haunts and there is a brooding quiet all about us. The Surveyor has been warned to stop work, and there would seem to be a silent but firm attempt to "freeze out," as the Cook says, all Government officials. The Interpreter betrayed to her this morning that, if "Washington" persisted in holding the new Agent here, the Indians would ask him to resign.

"And what if he does not?" she inquired.

James has a peculiar habit of going down on one knee and putting his hat upon the other when under any stress of emotion. He went down now and looking up at the Cook, said, "The Nez Perces mean business."

The purpose, as far as we can learn, is to remove the children from the schools, for the Agency policemen to go to their homes, and every Indian to keep out of sight. What will follow depends upon the action of the Agent and the news from Washington.

Reports have reached us that last night another secret council was held, four miles up the valley, at which Yellow Bull, one of the leaders in the last Nez Perce war, was present.[7] As he, with Chief Joseph, came out of that war surfeited with fighting, we hope his influence now may be for patience and peace.

A borderman has told us that the messenger to Washington went off on horseback, waving his arms as he rode away over the hills to Lewiston, and crying out, "If I do not get justice for my people, I will not come back to see the old men wrap their blankets over their heads and walk away from me."

We have been told, as an example of the tyranny complained of at the hands of the Agent, that an old grandfather, whose little girl was ill at the school, went for the child and carried her home in his arms. The Agent rode after him, tore the child away and put the grandfather in irons. The child

"The Author," Jane Gay *(Schlesinger Library, Radcliffe College)*

"Her Majesty, the Allotting Agent," from crayon drawing of Alice Fletcher by E. H. Miller, 1888 (*Peabody Museum, Harvard University*)

Fort Lapwai (*Idaho Historical Society*)

Joe Briggs, the surveyor, loading up the wagon (*Idaho Historical Society*)

"James, his mother and sister": James Stuart, Nancy Parsons, and Susanna Holmes (*Idaho Historical Society*)

"Lapwai church" (*Idaho Historical Society*)

Kate McBeth and group of Nez Perce women at the First Presbyterian Church, Lapwai (*Idaho Historical Society*)

"Camp McBeth," Kamiah. Alice Fletcher, Joe Briggs, and James Stuart on front step (*Idaho Historical Society*)

died that night and the old man was fined five dollars "for abducting a school-girl."

The Indian who told the story said, "it was a very old grandfather and a very little girl."

30th inst.

Judge Wilton, the interregnum Agent, has just informed us that he has orders to turn over the government property to the new appointee and Her Majesty decides to leave Lapwai. To avoid complications with the new officials, on whose account we are being boycotted, it is thought best to go as far as possible into the interior and camp among the Indians themselves. They say the quarrel is not with us, but as we are part of the government, we must wait until their grievances are settled. We are spending our fourth Sunday on the Reservation in anything but a peaceful state of mind, as befits the day. We are "to move tomorrow" and tomorrow is inevitable. We feel its steady approach every minute of this hot, dry Sunday.

Our friend the Missionary has told us that the progressive Indians have their homes in Kamiah, sixty-five miles distant. "Kamiah is a Paradise," said the Missionary, and we have determined to go to Paradise. You shall hear from us there. Do not let the newspapers make you anxious. I have just read in one that there is "serious trouble with the Nez Perces" and that the white settlers in the neighborhood are calling for troops. All the more reason for us to go to Paradise. We do not apprehend any trouble at present.

The Photographer, who has a way we do not all possess of getting at things, tells us that James Reuben, the messenger to Washington, was instructed to find out whether Her Majesty really represented the Government, and if what she says is true, that the Indians must take their lands in severalty.[8] A Portland paper states that James Reuben is "pleading manfully in Washington for his people, but so far with no success." He has once before pled for his people and won his cause. It was in 1885, when Joseph's band of surrendered warriors were rapidly dying out with homesickness and disease in the Indian Territory, where they had been sent by the Government in 1877.

James had gone among the captives out of "pity for the children who were growing up in ignorance" and he gathered them into a school, teaching them what he could. But he soon realized that in a very short time there would be none to teach. He decided to go to Washington and plead in their behalf. His eloquence prevailed and he was allowed to bring the remnant of the band home. It had dwindled from four hundred and eighteen souls to one hundred and eighteen. Our interpreter's wife, Harriet, was one of the children he brought back.

You can imagine what an influence James Reuben has with his people. He is also very popular among the white settlers in the adjoining towns, and is invited to give the oration on the 4th of July celebrations. I hope you may meet him, if you have not already done so, in Washington.

Letter Four

SQUIRREL CAMP
July 15th, 1889

The unexpected has happened; it has actually rained! It was at Lapwai. We were all packed, ready for starting on the morrow in search of our Indian, when, on the 30th of June, while the wagon stood at the door of our quarters, a cloud no bigger than a man's hand appeared in the west. James detected it first and gave us warning and ran for the tarpaulin. We all went out and watched the most wonderful growth of that cloud, momentarily more and more threatening, its black billows, with now and then a spasmodic glow of fire in the heart of it, rolling on in rapid tumult, until at length it burst over our heads and the deluge came. Our thermometer fell from 102° to 70° and the chickens rose up out of their dust wallows and closed their gaping bills; the dog crawled out from under the house and sniffed the air eagerly; Gooey threw wide open all the windows of our quarters and the Cook was restrained only by force from standing bareheaded out in the blessed rain.

In twelve hours the dust was flying as briskly as before, and with our belongings all dried, we were again ready to start. We rose at dawn and set out at five o'clock on the morning of July 1st. The pine wood of the porch, as we stepped upon it, was literally broiling in the rays of the sun, so that our feet stuck in the pitch that exuded from the boards. The acting Agent had kindly allowed us to take, for the trip, the Webster wagon and the team of work horses, to carry our camp outfit. It was a tentative outfit; for, aside from the tent itself, we scarcely knew what we should require. We had no settled ideas about "Paradise"; not even in the matter of clothing. . . .

We had been told before we left Washington, that the climate of Idaho was delightful, but so far nothing resembling delight had been developed in any member of our party. By day our blood rushed through our parboiled arteries; by night, four double blankets had hardly prevented its congealing. The still incomplete process of acclimation had been trying to us all, but especially so to the Cook, who had hitherto proved herself to be of the even tempered sort, and to the Photographer, who, we all knew, was not a blow hot, blow cold, sort of friend. It had even been mildly disturbing to Her Majesty to oscillate from overcoat to gossamer clothing many times a day, according to the height of the sun above the horizon.

* * *

But we were all packed at last, after much deliberation and a good deal of difference of opinion,—our tent, our trunk containing winter clothing and our trunk of summer apparel; the Cook's hopeful but untried stove, her tin and her wooden ware, our canned tomatoes and our coal-oil can, our corn beef and lucifer matches, flour bags and groceries, our axe and umbrella, our potatoes and salt, Her Majesty's bobbin of red tape, the Photographer's tripod and camera, and—Briggs' dog.

We bowled out of the Agency inclosure in fine style, the Special Agent driving Dick and Jimmy, radiant in their new harness, and her Cook, Photographer and friend perched upon the miscellaneous freight in her wagon.

The Driver and Interpreter followed with the loaded Webster wagon, and the Surveyor, with a head on his shoulders and a heart buttoned up in his blue jeans blouse, came last with his span of ancient but quite respectable horses, attached to what, in western parlance, is called a buggy, being an open box wagon. The buggy was packed fore and aft with the Surveyor's camp belongings, over which his much-the-worse-for-wear canvas tent-cloth was corded, while his coffee pot hung behind in company with his iron camp kettle. There was no holiday look about the Surveyor or his outfit; it was all for honest work, and we felt a thrill of confidence in our own integrity as we glanced backward and beheld his team plunging on with an inspiring directness of purpose.

At the end of the first quarter of a mile we suddenly stopped, for the weight of our load had forced the brake block down upon the wheel and locked it. Fortunately the axe was *not* in the bottom of the wagon, thanks to the Cook, who has a way of putting things "where they will be handy." We cut off an inch of the block and went on. Our big off horse Dick is pigeon-toed, with elephantine hoofs and ankles to correspond, and we grew dizzy trying to analyze the resultant motion of his feet; he got over the ground so much quicker than his mate Jimmy that our driver said we ought to have some eveners.

He told us that an evener is a stout strap to hold the double-tree and single-tree together in such a way that one horse cannot run away with his side of the wagon against the will of the other horse. Your Majesty thought that some such contrivance should be applicable to partnerships in general and entered the suggestion in her notebook.

Our way lay over Craig's Mountain; the ascent was of the roughest and our loads heavy. The poor beasts did their best, but they toiled painfully up the winding road which hugs the mountainside. Now the Special Agent is brave in general. There is not a fibre of moral cowardice in her constitution, but, as we turned a sharp corner and found ourselves hanging on the very verge of a precipice with a rocky climb just before us, and Dick stopped short and then began to back, the foundations of her faith gave way beneath her, and she stayed not upon the order of her going. All that the Photographer could clearly state, when we afterwards talked it over, was that he had a drop-shutter impression of a swiftly moving object in mid-air and an instantaneous view of the possibilities which lay at the bottom of the abyss on one side, the adamantine trap wall upon the other and the rugged ascent in front, upon which the horses seemed to be suspended by the neck and struggling to gain a foothold. The Cook said she saw something jump, as it were, out of the frying pan into the fire, and she confessed that she felt a monentary sense of betrayal, a consciousness of being deserted, when a sharp cut upon Dick's haunches and the imperative voice of James our Driver and Interpreter, arrested the backsliding team and prompted it to a vigorous effort to regain lost ground. Then we steadied our nerves by a climb on foot, and at the top of the hill the Special Agent gathered up herself and the lines and we went on until nightfall found us beside a spring of pure water, where cattle were loitering for their evening draught.

It was a pretty place. A little line of green herbage along the trickling stream was restful to our sunburnt eyes, and we pitched our tent under a lofty pine tree and fried our potatoes and boiled our coffee over crackling thorn bushes. . . .

The next day, the same broiling sun, the same burnt grass under the horses' feet where it was not sharp broken trap rock. We toiled on, stopping an hour at noon to rest the horses and to eat a bit of cold beef and bread, for it was too warm to wish for our usually indispensable coffee.

We arrived at the top of Craig's Mountain and the temperature dropped as the daylight waned: we did not know how much, but when our tent was pitched, we shivered at its whiteness, and rejoiced when the Surveyor touched a match to a pine tree and the flame ran swiftly up the pitchy bark. We struggled into our overcoats and crouched within the radius of its warmth while all the time there was an unpleasant creeping up and down our spinal column. In the morning there was ice in the water bucket and hoar frost stiffened our tent cloth. We pushed on toward the little hamlet of Cottonwood and pitched our tent by the roadside, while the sun was still high above the horizon. James wanted to shoe his horses and the Surveyor had to identify an important corner monument of the original treaty survey of the Reservation and to trace an old line eastward. Here we had our first enlightenment as to the habits of the indigenous horse. Ours disappeared during the night. . . .

While in camp, waiting for James to bring back our truant horses, some more cattlemen called upon us. They made a very short call and now the Photographer says that Her Majesty is not popular with the cattlemen.

When James returned with Dick and Jimmy, the Cook asked him how much farther it was to Kamiah and something he said gave us pain. He said we had gone over pretty much all the *road* there was. He guessed he could take us down, but he did not know how the wagons would stand it. By dint of much ingenuity expended in the severest anthropological research of her life, Her Majesty at last came to the facts, I might say, the bottom facts of the situation, though the Surveyor said the fact was a cañon and the "bottom had dropped out."

Yes; Paradise lay at the water level on the Clearwater River, a sheer descent of 2500 feet. So far our way had been as rough as a political campaign, but now we were told there was no road whatever and that we must just tumble bodily down a cañon. . . .

There was a little cabin just ahead, over the line, and the Surveyor proposed a halt for reconnoissance. The cabin was a rough, unfinished board box, but it had a roof that would cast a shade and for miles and miles there had not been a shadow of tree or rock and we were hot and weary and glad of the cabin; it was better than our white tent. . . .

After a luxurious supper of coffee, potatoes, corned beef

and bread, we held a protracted meeting with our driver and interpreter and succeeded in drawing out of him all that he knew about the way to Paradise. And then we wrapped the drapery of our camp bed about us and lay down to unconscious celebration. We had several hundred pounds of "outfit" and a six months' supply of provisions upon our burdened soul; we comprehended even in our sleep that it was one thing to roll a loaded Webster wagon down a cañon and quite another thing to pull it up. If we should, by any happy concatenation of events, be able to catch our Indian and should want to climb out of that subterranean Paradise and find a new point of departure, the question of hoisting a ton or more of subsistence would be a grave one. . . .

Before morning our mind was made up to cache half our provisions, to send back to the Agency the Webster wagon, our big trunk and sundry other impedimenta, and upon James' return to go on in light marching order. . . .

While we have been awaiting our driver's return from the Agency, we have made a flying trip to Mount Idaho, a small village in a picturesque tangle of the fringe of civilization; all beyond being mining region. Here we found another Missionary, Miss Sue McBeth, sister of our friend at Lapwai. She had made a home in the border settlement to escape the persecutions of the officials on the Reservation. She was charged with inciting the Nez Perces to insubordination. What she actually did was, forseeing the changes which were so rapidly coming upon them, she tried to teach her pupils something of the nature of the United States' government and laws, and, unfortunately, she began with the Declaration of Independence.

From what we know of Miss Sue, we are confident that she did not deliberately plan the subversion of the Agency System. We are more inclined to believe that she did not apprehend the pernicious nature of the document in question. She made no defense, but took refuge in Mt. Idaho, bought a little house, which has become the headquarters of righteousness for the whole neighborhood, and hither the Indians come and are taught the ways of God unmolested. No driving storm or biting cold can stay their ponies' steady tramp when their faces are set toward this sanctuary among the Mountains.

We returned to Squirrel's camp to find that James had just come from Lapwai, with Harriet, his wife; our first intimation that when we hire an Indian, in any capacity, his wife is included in the bargain; where he goeth, she will go—if she pleases,—but no marital bond is strong enough to take her against her own will.

Tomorrow, we go to Kamiah, our Paradise, if the horses are not missing when we wake. . . .

Letter Five

KAMIAH
July 18, 1889

While we were detained at Squirrel's camp, we made the acquaintance of the settlers in the neighborhood. They were kind and courteous and offered to assist us in any way within their power, and we visited several of their farms. We were told that the land was poor, that two crops out of five seasons was all that could be expected and that several of the largest farmers were trying to sell their places and go west. Discouragement was visible everywhere and an expression of hopelessness upon the faces of the women, at which, when we came to think of their condition, we did not wonder. Briggs said, "This country is good enough for cattle and men, but it is death on women and horses." As in these days of machine plows and cultivators, it is the horses and women that do the hard work of a farm, Briggs may not be far wrong in his rough estimate, but when we talked with the women, they did not complain of the work, but only of the lonesome life they led.

The men can jump upon their ponies and ride off to see a man whenever the social instinct prompts. When wearied in the contemplation of nature, from his vantage point on the seat of a McCormick Reaper, a man can ride on to the neighborhood store and perch himself upon a box or barrel, light his pipe, and talk for half a day with Tom, Dick and Harry, who are also relieving the tedium of their lives and enlarging the scope of their ideas in the interchange of opinions. . . . But diversions are not for the frontier woman unless she is an Indian woman. *She* can jump upon her pony and ride away whenever she chooses. The children are no hindrance. She can hang them up in a tree, to wait her return, or she will tie the cradle-board to her saddle and gallop off as free as her husband; freer, indeed, for she *owns* her children, her horses, her home and all its belongings. Her Majesty says, "The Indian woman can take down the tent, if she so pleases, and depart with all her property, leaving the man to sit helpless upon the ground; for the husband is only a guest in the lodge of the wife."

You see, . . . that civilization has been built up largely upon the altruism of the woman, at the cost of her independence; and is still an expensive luxury to her.

* * *

Squirrel's Camp had begun to feel like a home when the day came that we must leave its hospitable roof. We rose before the fading of the morning star and ate our breakfast in the cool of the dawn, but, when we had packed our diminished belongings and pulled out towards the much desired bourne, the sun streamed down upon our heads like veritable arrows of fire. The Cook hung the coffee pot in its rays at the tailboard of the wagon, where "it would be hot when wanted," and the Photographer grumbled about the softening of his gelatine plates. But Briggs was as "cool as a cucumber in a cold frame"; anything less than 120° in the shade was beneath his notice. James had the lines and he drove out over the land, unbroken save by deeply worn cattle trails. The horses kicked up the alkaline dust in a cloud which excoriated our faces, blinded our eyes and parched our lips. We looked through our smoked glasses, straining our vision to catch the first glimpse of Paradise. All day we thought of green pastures and still waters, and all day we traversed wide stretches of burnt prairie where the soil was thin and the growth scanty, over rocky wastes and sharp pitches up and down, passing now and then patches of better land which a reliable supply of water might convert into fruitful fields. Just as the day was waning, a cloud spread out from the west and surged over the burning sky. It had an angry look, but Briggs said that summer clouds in Idaho were harmless bravado. We were trying to put implicit confidence in the Surveyor when the team stopped and James told us to get down; we must walk the rest of the way.

We found ourselves on the brink of a sharp descent. We looked over the edge, and lo! the vale of Kamiah lay at our feet.

We saw the Clearwater River, running like a silver line through the cañon, narrowing here and broadening there and the shadows of the swiftly moving clouds giving the whole valley a strange weird coloring.

There was a rumble of thunder in the distance behind us, then a vivid flash and a crash among the tall trees whose tops were beneath our feet, and the wind rushed like an army of ghosts past us down into the cañon. The long arms of the firs waved to and fro and the rushing sound echoed and re-echoed and rose and fell over the plains, hills, and valleys, dying in a sob, only to rise again as waves of the sea break and gather and beat upon the shore.

Her Majesty's hat struggled in the gale for freedom and we held to the wagon wheels to steady ourselves. James told us to go along the ridge of the bare mountain upon whose summit we were, and we blindly obeyed. We saw no path, only a slight trail which we followed until we reached a spot where the trail was lost on a wide expanse of trap rock. The wind took us off our feet; the mountain sloped at an angle of—well, we did not measure the angle; we only knew that if we went down any farther we must roll down. We threw ourselves upon the rock to keep from being blown off the ridge and her Majesty said, "We must go back and follow the team; where the horses can go, we can follow. We are not flies that we can crawl over the sharp edges of the mountain." While the rest of us were thinking that, if we were flies, we would use our wings in this dilemma, we caught sight of the teams plunging down a ravine to the left of our position. In our bird's-eye view, the horses were invisible under the wagons. The wheels were locked and slid gratingly over the stones in a manner that prophesied their disintegration before the gates of Paradise could be reached.

We turned and scrambled into the gulch, pitching like a storm-tossed vessel, now head fore-most, anon with broadside on, and lodging against a tall tree just as a serpentine flash of lightning cleft the sky and a sharp report of thunder put new vigor into the limbs of the Cook who declared with what health she had left that she never could abide trees in a storm.

We should never have known the rate of motion our Cook was capable of but for that storm. She is not slow at any time, but her progress that day was simply phenomenal. Her Majesty, trying in vain to keep pace with her, realized at length that one must enter Paradise alone, and so, half famishing and wholly exhausted, she came upon the disjointed members of her party at the bottom of the cañon and sat down upon the trunk of a fallen tree to recover breath and strength. Her garments were wet and mud-stained, her eyes were dimmed with congestion, her hands and feet cold, and she shivered in general discomfort.

The Cook, arrived before her long enough to feel a reaction from her exalted energy, looked embarrassed and expressed anxiety as to Her Majesty's welfare. . . .

And thus we entered Kamiah. The clouds rolled away and the blue sky was reflected in the Clearwater. The valley lay like a haven of rest and peace, lovely in the rain washed atmosphere but so very silent. Not a sound greeted us as we came out of the gulch upon the shore of the silver stream. There was a ferry boat which would carry one team at a time and the driver and the surveyor poled us over. A few cows standing near the landing place ceased chewing the cud for a moment to stare at us. A piebald pony in a fenced field with alert ears and curious eyes stood with his head over the top rail, trying to make us out. But the cows uttered no sound and the pony was dumb. There was not even a chattering magpie to greet us. We were unwelcomed and unexpected.

We passed a log cabin or two as we drove along the riverside, but no one waited at the door for us. Special Indian Agents are but human and Her Majesty was oppressed. Homesickness was stealing over her, and she closed her eyes to the beauty of the landscape. Its loveliness did not compensate for what it lacked. There was no soul in it for her and she reached back for the clasp of the hand of a far-away friend. It steadied her to grasp even in imagination, something that was her own for here she was indeed a stranger in a strange land.

A sigh came from the Cook at her side. She had forgotten the Cook. Was it possible that she too suffered from nostalgia? Another sigh, and Her Majesty asked, "What is it?" with as much feeling in the voice as she could spare from herself.

Now if that Cook were forty fathoms down in the dumps she would speak only of—well! dumplings, perhaps. She is of the kind that would "let concealment like a worm i' the bud prey on her damask cheek" for the term of her natural life and then have cheek enough left to deny the worm. So when asked the meaning of that sigh, she unblushingly said, "I wonder if there are fish in the river. It would be nice to have a fry for supper.". . .

When Her Majesty smiled on the Cook, that craven soul believed that the foretaste of her impossible fry was at the bottom of the smile and her conscience was troubled at the effect of her disingenuousness; for did she not know beyond a peradventure that nothing less than a miracle could substitute for that night or for many and many another either the fowls of the air or the fish of the sea for the inevitable tin-canned diet of a United States Special Indian Agent.

But Her Majesty was feasting on ambrosia then and she smiled again on the Cook and asked the driver what that small board cabin just coming in sight might be? There was a chimney at one end made of stones and sticks and mud, a rail fence surrounded it, mullein stalks grew among the burnt grass in the yard and there was some sort of curtain over the western window, and three magpies sat on the wooden steps.

"Who lives there?"

"Oh," said the Driver, "that's where we are going." He took down a section of the worn fence, and drove into the enclosure. The door yielded to a strong hand and we entered.

It was but a "poor bit place"—three little rooms, but the spirit of the good Missionary whose home it had been for many years seemed still within its walls.

The Surveyor dumped his cargo in the outer room and the Special Agent's effects were piled up in a heap upon the floor of the inner one. The horses were turned loose and we were left to evoke order out of confusion. . . .

Letter Six

Kamiah
July 26th, 1889

. . . Since I last wrote, we have crossed our Rubicon, which was a mountain, and are now settled deep down in a cañon through which runs the Clearwater River. The Indians call the valley Kamiah and they speak the word as if it were a well beloved name. In their legends the Kamiah valley is the birth place of the Nez Perce. Some mysterious monster was killed here by the coyote and from the drops of his blood sprang the people. There is a mound shaped hill in the valley which they say is the heart of the Coyote.[9]

Kamiah is to be our home for the remainder of the summer, and the center of our operations. True, the tent must lie ready to be unfolded at a moment's notice, but we have set up, for the nonce, our household goods in this little board cabin; Camp McBeth, we call it, in honor of its owner, Miss McBeth, known to you as the devoted missionary whose works not only do follow her, but also stay behind to leaven the whole Nez Perce tribe. She has sent us from Mt. Idaho, where she now resides, a welcome to her house and a "God bless you" on our work. How can we but start out hopefully?

Picture us if you can! Our cabin is framed, with one thickness of board nailed upright on the outside. Originally the edges of these boards probably touched each other but they do not now, so we do not lack good ventilation.

We have three rooms and a woodshed and are in a palace for our cabin not only contains the necessities for right living but furnishes food for the aesthetic part of our nature. Our bric-a-brac ornaments are tin cans whose highly colored labels minister to the pride of the eye, the tomato contributing the warm tints and the salmon the cool liquid ideas. Hung along on the walls are not pictures to stimulate the imagination but solid facts to forestall it. Bags of unbleached muslin soft in tone, and tied with contrasting red tape, contain our sugar, flour and dried fruit. Our camp bed is ornamental in blue blankets, and the striped "cloes bag" you wrote of stands out in bold relief against the yellow pine walls. How do you like our color scheme?

Outside there are a few stunted pine trees, too far away to intercept the rays of the sun, and there is a spring a quarter of a mile distant which contributes to our water supply. We shall not gather about our centre table in the cool of the day and no student's lamp will burn for us. We are glad that we have no centre table and no student's lamp; we sigh only for a little darkness. It is glare, glare, glare until our eyes are scorched and we long for the midnight hours which are all too short when finally they do wrap a semi-luminous veil about us. . . .

We are next neighbor, within a mile, to a milch cow, an unlooked for blessing. The cow's owner has agreed to supply us with a quart of milk daily so long as the cow season lasts. She is old "Kentucky's" wife. "Kentucky"[10] is a policeman and his wife a neat kindly body who never fails to bring a beaming smile and a hearty good morning (Tots-ka-lawa) with her well polished tin pail.

We have in our abode two chairs of native construction.

They are a solid foundation so long as we carefully occupy them, but tumble over backward whenever we rise. They are painted sky blue, mellowed by age and the abrasions of hard usage. They were evidently modeled upon the church pew. If you can conceive of a pew so constructed that the two ends approach within eighteen inches of each other, you have the picture of our chairs. . . .

We are practically alone here. The Surveyor has gone to Lewiston for a day or two and our driver and interpreter has his camp half a mile distant. We are at peace with our world for our world is too small to be divided upon any subject whatever. . . .

In a few weeks time we shall go out again under the tent and the Indians will come and there will be camp fires at night to gossip beside and human nature to study with no conventional hindrances. These bits of free life will linger as lovely pictures in your old friend's mind long after the privations are forgotten. . . .

[From an enclosed letter for her correspondent's daughter:]

. . . A little way from our cabin is a big hill which the Indians call "Bear's Claws." I send you a picture of it, and you can see the claws if you look long enough.

Indians have some queer notions and it is not always easy to tell where they get them. Lately they have been bringing me their children to photograph "because they were going to die."

"Looking Glass'" daughter brought her little boy a few weeks ago. He was a roly poly little fellow and I said I did not think he was going to die. "Oh yes," the Mother said, he was; so I made a picture for her and sure enough, the little boy died soon after. "Looking Glass" was an old chief, a great warrior, and his daughter is a nice pretty woman, as you will see. Do you notice that Indians have beautifully shaped hands?

Today is Sunday and ponies are tied about under the pine trees for the Indians have come to church. They come early and stay all day, the whole family, babies and dogs included,

41

and they picnic outside our rail fence and I catch "snaps" now and then of pretty little groups in the grass. An Indian preaches but we cannot understand what he says. I think he tells the people that they must not do any work on Sunday if they want to go to heaven, for you cannot persuade one of them to do anything for you on that day. Our boy never came near us this morning to see if we were alive or needed water from the spring. It would have been wicked and so the Surveyor had to bring the buckets. . . .

Letter Seven

KAMIAH
August 17th 1889

When I last wrote you, we had just tumbled down into this peaceful valley. Peaceful it has proved to be, but to us, that night, it seemed as if we had fallen upon chaos.

When the door closed upon the retiring form of the Surveyor, the candle he had left, stuck in a black bottle, flared in the draft and then cast a dim radius of light upon the scene. There upon the floor in indescribable confusion lay our bags and boxes of supplies, camp paraphernalia, packs, saddles and the harness of the horses. . . .

The Cook said afterwards that she could have wept but for her New England education, which had taught her that salvation was to be obtained only in doing what she did not want to do, and that human happiness, for the most part, consisted in cheerful martyrdom. Bodily fatigue had overpowered the pangs of hunger, and all these two wanted was a place in which to lie down and forget their woe, for the numbness that precedes sleep was stealing over them as they sat among their demoralized household goods.

A mysterious scrambling noise close at hand and a fall of

some unknown body startled them. The Cook sprang to her feet and seized the butcher knife. A scratching as if some living thing was forcing its way up the thin boards of the cabin "curdled the blood in her veins," so she said the next day. All she did now was to open a door and grope her way along a narrow passage leading to the back of the cabin. A troop of mice fled before her, and she passed out into the wood-shed, a dark object rushed by and disappeared in the gloom.

The stumbling upon a pile of nicely cut pine wood at her very feet roused her dormant energies and she returned with an armful, kindled a fire in the capacious chimney, and a hot cup of coffee soon revived the drooping spirits so that when Briggs looked in after caring for his own camp, speech was once more possible.

A night's repose upon the hardest of couches, broken only by the circling of bats over our heads and the occasional repetition of the scratching noise outside; an awakening at dawn, hastened by the chatter of magpies and the tapping of woodpeckers in the pine boarding; and we were ready for the work of the new day.

While the Special Agent arranged the outer room for an office, the Cook explored the pantry and the Photographer went in search of a dark room. From time to time the labors of Her Majesty were interrupted by bulletins from the Cook who was developing a mine of treasures left by the blessed little missionary when she was driven from her home here in the Kamiah Valley.

"Here is a real stone jar," called out the Cook.

The Allotting Agent was deep in the abstruse calculations respecting the quantity of forage for the next quarter. The Cook jarred upon her nerves, as she burst in with a shout of triumph, bearing a white crockery wash-bowl:

"By the manes of the great unwashed! look at this!"

"Yes! Yes!," groans the Special Agent, who is trying now to wash her hands of some old agency complications; trying to understand how to catch her Indian. . . .

And so our first day in Kamiah drew slowly to its close. While the more pronounced members of her family are gradually settling down into quietness which becomes the twilight hour, Her Majesty opens the outer door and looks out into the depths of the clear sky. A feathery cloud hangs over the mountain down which we came, is it but one day since?. . .

There is no human tone in the night's melody and with the unsolved problem still in her brain, the Special Agent sighs, when, out from under the steps upon which she sits, a pole-cat emerges and waddles like a duck, here and there about her feet. He is rather pretty to look at. The white stripe along his back catches the expiring light of day and his tail waves like a plume in its departing rays.

All forms of nature are inspiring to the observant soul. Her Majesty starts from her pensive attitude and there is newborn energy in her step as she comes into the house and shuts the door with unwonted evolution of force. . . .

In the days that followed that "wild beast" and Her Majesty grew to be fast friends. He came out of the darkness of night through our doorway, himself as black as the night, with eyes like balls of fire. He made straight for the Cook, who picked him up by the neck. If she had any murderous intent, she relented when the little imp cuddled up in her arms and purred gently.

"How very soft its fur is," said she, as she handed the creature to the Allotting Agent, who adopted it for her very own and they have been inseparable friends ever since. If she goes for a walk, he follows in her wake, sedately, with head erect, or prances on before, with tail snapping with feline enjoyment, stopping now and then and looking back to be sure that she is near. If she sits down between the box stove and the kerosene lamp, he sits down in the same chair, and with the same content and the same purr of satisfaction for the limited creature comforts of the situation. He grows gentle in her company and his aristocratic tail waves more and more gracefully as the acquaintance ripens into true fellowship.

* * *

The sun looked in through the small windows of our cabin upon that Sunday morning and found us all stilled with the thought of what might be the outcome of the day's endeavor. Her Majesty walked out, unbonneted, to drink in the peace of the hour. How still it was! One could catch the tramp of a horse coming up the valley long before the animal came into view. Nearer and nearer, and she hears the splashing of the water at the ford and the rattling of the stones, and up the bank out upon the open trail there rides an Indian on a dappled pony, then another,—a woman—, with a baby tied to a board at her side, then two boys on one horse, then a group of women and half dozen men following; the women clad in bright-colored shawls and handkerchiefs tied about the head, the men with blankets before them on the horse; some wearing linen coats, some in flannel shirts, all moving sedately on, mindful of the day; the dogs which followed alone seeming unawed by the fourth commandment; and still they came, in twos and threes, the women riding together, the men apart.

There was subdued excitement in our camp. The Cook came out to see and the photographer dusted his camera.

"What a delicious bit," said he, "that woman with the three children strung around her on that piebald pony."

The procession passes and the Indians dismount and tie the horses among the low pine trees.

The women sit together in groups on the yellow grass near the door of a little "Church House," which, half hidden by the branches, stands just behind, on the left of our cabin, and the men gather together and talk quietly.

What can they talk about? Suddenly a bell startles the still atmosphere. The sound does not fall upon us, it creeps along the ground, for there is no belfry on the church. The bell is in a box behind the building and an Indian is striking it with a stick. It answers the purpose. The Indians rise and enter the church, the women first, then the men.

The Special Agent crosses the sunburnt field and goes in also and there, clustered on benches, on the floor, packed close together, she finds the Christian Kamiah Indians. There they sit in reverent silence, weary with the troubled little world they know, dull with the poverty of it, hardly comprehending, but still finding comfort in the promise of a better chance in the world to come.

It was not easy to look unmoved into those dark faces. The preacher was an Indian, the service was in Nez Perce, with a psalm read in English and a hymn or two. The Cook, listening outside, heard the words queerly twirled about the Nez Perce tongue.

> I need Thee, oh, I need Thee,
> Every hour I need Thee."

They were wailed out in the reedy notes of the women, the deep tones of the men and the thin voices of the children. And the song floated across to Briggs, who lay under a pine tree, and he rose and strolled over to the church. He came back half an hour later and told the Cook that, after the service, Her Majesty talked to the Indians "like a man and a brother."

"My land!" said he, "I couldn't help it." The Cook did not ask what it was that Briggs couldn't help; she saw it in his eye, but she put on her hat and went over and looked in at the church door.

Away up over the heads of the people she saw, at the end of the room, a double row of little children sitting on the steps of the pulpit platform as if pinned down right to it. They were as immovable as a row of wax dolls; no wiggling about, no crowding. There they sat, looking demurely straight before them, their little moccasined feet turned in and their small brown hands lying together in their laps.

Indian children are exemplary. I have yet to see them quarrel. Perhaps they have inherited the hopelessness of fighting. There is something uncanny about the silent way they look at you out of their big, black eyes; you would feel better if you could see a brisk wrestle and a tumble in earnest; a little healthy hair pulling match. . . .

Before the Indians separated, the Allotting Agent asked them to meet her at the Church the following day. They made no response, it is not their way, and we could not know that twenty-five miles distant, in Mount Idaho, a lonely, banished woman, whom the Kamians call "Our Mother," had been working for us with her Indian children all the troubled days since we first crossed the Reservation line, nor could we have guessed that in the morning prayer in the Kamiah church house, in an Indian tongue, we had been remembered, but Her Majesty felt that here at last she had found her vantage point.

* * *

We all awoke that Monday morning as if a new responsibility had been laid upon us during the night, which had not yet been satisfactorily adjusted to our shoulders. Even Briggs had a subdued air about him inconsistent with the rollicking expression of his hat, and the Cook placed the breakfast upon the table in unwonted silence. She had taken especial pains in its preparation, for whenever the Cook is under any stress of emotion, whatever she does is sure to feel the force of it. . . .

Her Majesty's cheeks were flushed. . . . Hitherto she had been trying to solve a simple problem, how to find her point d'appui; now that the opportunity had come, how to make no mistake at the outset which might mar all her future endeavors? I dare say the rest of us felt her responsibility more than she did herself, for we had less knowledge and more anxiety. She was concerned for her work; we had *that* and Her Majesty herself upon our minds and the Cook, who was bound to see that her part was not slurred in its performance, began to realize the complexity of her task.

And Briggs was restless; he went in and out of the cabin whistling "Jerusalem the golden," and finally disappeared. He would meet us at the church, he said.

The Photographer puts a fresh plate in his camera and sets up his tripod in the yard, and the Interpreter nervously ties and unties again a knot in his handkerchief, then goes out and disturbs the magpies on the steps who fly up and dart down again upon the window-sill and carry off the Cook's long-handled dish mop and then as if they also had undertaken too big a task, they drop it outside the fence and fly away over the pine trees. By eight o'clock the tramp of the ponies' feet and the yelping of dogs were portentous sounds in our ears.

Presently the Interpreter comes in and says, "The people are all ready," then the bell rings for them to go into the church and they file in silently filling the small building from pulpit to doorway. They are all men, the women staying at home in an exemplary manner, just like civilized white women when any matter particularly affecting their interests is being discussed by the men.

Her Majesty put on her broad-brimmed straw hat and took a straight line to the church and Briggs emerged from the shade of the pine trees and wandered over in a zigzag fashion as if quite unconcerned. As for the Cook, she felt that her place was in the reserve corps. If the rest fell back upon her, as they generally did in an emergency, she would be ready and equal to the occasion.

The Photographer ventured as far as the steps to the church and sat down beside his camera. He came over now and then to report progress to the Cook.

"They are not pleasant to look at," said he, on his first round; "some of the old ones scowled as Her Majesty passed by them into the church."

"They all scowl," said the Cook; "it is the sun in their faces; you cannot tell simply by that."

Meanwhile the Allotting Agent had passed up to the pulpit through the dusky throng. No hand had been held out to her, no smile had greeted her entrance. She turned and faced the rows of silent men. The Interpreter stood beside her. He was working his fingers nervously and his eyes wandered weakly over the crowd.

We did not know it then, but he had been threatened with "punishment" if he remained in the service of Her Majesty. Old men that very day had tried to terrorize him and young men had warned him of the fate which was hanging over his head. Briggs knew, and he sauntered carelessly up and stood beside Her Majesty.

"My land!," said he to the Cook afterwards. "I was all of a tremble inside and there *she* stood just as calm and smiling as if she was teaching a primary department of a mission Sunday School down East. Nothing exciting about it."

She stood looking straight before her a few minutes until there was absolute silence in the room, and then she said, "My friends, this is God's house and what we are to talk about is a serious matter, affecting the lives and happiness of all; your lives, and the lives of your wives and children. It is right to ask God's blessing here in this house, that all we do may please Him." Then she turned and said a few words to the native Pastor who rose and spoke in Nez Perce. The Photographer said that as he went on the scowls relaxed a little and one or two of them said "amen" (A-a-h) at the end.

Then the Allotting Agent explained what she had called them together to hear: explained the land allotment, the meaning of citizenship and her wish that the whole people would see the wisdom of the great change that she had come to bring upon them and would help her in her work.

Still a silence, but one man was taking notes on a bit of paper.

The Interpreter read the law and then sat down and waited. A little stir arose among the people, two or three whispered together, and at length one man stood up, a tall, broad-shouldered fellow with a deep voice and an air of authority about him. He was Kip-ka-pal-i-kan, a United States official, having been appointed Judge of the Indian Court of Offences.[11] He said, "We do not want our land cut up in little pieces; we have not told you to do it. We must wait for our people in Lapwai to consent."

The Special Agent does not understand this, but learns in the days that follow that the Lapwai Indians, suspecting her to be an imposter, had sent word to the Kamiahs to have nothing done until the return of the messenger who had gone to Washington.

They could scarcely be blamed for their incredulity; that reasonable human beings, thought worthy of having citizenship thrust upon them, should have no voice what ever in matters which so exclusively concerned themselves, was an idea too difficult for the untutored mind to grasp.

In ignorance why the Nez Perce are determined to put off the work, why they thwart her all they can, the Allotting

Agent tells them now in the little church, that they must take their land in severalty, because it is the law and is best for them, but she wins no encouraging response.

However, there is a tone in Her Majesty's voice that begins to attract the unwilling ear. The Indians notice that she makes no promises,—they are sick of promises.

She tells them she has come to bring them manhood, that they may stand up beside the white man in equality before the law. The idea is hard to grasp. The prospect of standing beside the white man is not a very brilliant one. The unadulterated Indian looks *down* upon the species of white men he knows any thing about. As to the law, all they know about the law is, that it is some contrivance to get ponies and cattle and land out of the red man's possession into that of the white man; it is a one-sided machine; it never brings back an Indian's stolen horse, or takes the border ruffian's fence or his cattle off the Indian's land. If to be equal before the law could mean a chance for the Indian! A few catch a glimmer of the possibility and their faces relax.

One old man stands up and says, "We are not able to go alone, our limbs tremble under us." He is afraid of he knows not what. Some of the young and strong look up with a new gleam in the eye and Briggs gives a sigh of relief as he sees the man who had been taking notes rise to ask some intelligent questions about the Severalty Act. Finally the invitation is given the Indians to call at the cabin and be registered and talk about the land.

"The women are to come also," said Her Majesty, "every man, woman and child in the tribe must have land. It is their inheritance."

The Pastor shakes hands with the Agent and a few of the men shyly come up and say "Tots-ka-lava", (good-morning) and so a crack for the entering wedge is opened.

The council over, the Photographer, waiting outside with his camera, catches the people as they group themselves about the door.

The Indians are pleased to have their photographs taken and some press forward to be in front while the Pastor modestly slips behind and is hidden in the shadows. The Photographer shows some of the old men the pictures on the ground glass, whereat they laugh and wonder. . . .

* * *

Robert Williams, the native Pastor of Kamiah, called to see Her Majesty the day following the Council in his church.[12] He was cordial in his greetings to which his halting English did scant justice. He had talked much with Miss McBeth about this new law and, said he, "I take my land now but my people not all understand yet."

So the big blank book was opened and Robert was registered and Robert's wife and the fathers and mothers of both and of brothers and sisters a goodly number. And the next day, "Old Billy,"[13] Robert's father, came and he made a new point of departure and Luke his brother started a new circle and then other Indians dropped in, one by one, at first as if it were a serious surgical operation to be registered; some as if ashamed to come and others as if afraid.

Before victory had made their politics respectable, the thirteen original "black Republicans" of Washington met after dark and expressed their opinions only behind closed doors. The Nez Perces of these first days were braver. They tied their ponies to our fence in broad daylight, knowing perfectly well what the consequences might be.

Ponies have sickened and died with less provocation. Needles thrust into the creatures' brain, as Indians know how to do, and left to rust there, is one of the punishments for whose who defy the old chiefs' power; corrals opened in the night and ponies allowed to wander off is another mode of expressing disapprobation of an Indian's conduct; the "medicine man's" incantation over his garden patch whereby his potatoes shrivel and rot and his cabbage refuses to head; spells laid upon his family, in consequence of which the children take measles or go blind with ophthalmia—these are real dangers to the Indian who dares think for himself and stand up under the tyranny of the old chiefs, who, blind and unscrupulous as they are, have sense enough to see their power waning and would use desperate means to hinder the inevitable. The progressive Indian has foes within the tribe, as well as enemies without, to fight and few of us know how hard the struggle is.

The Cook said "all the emotions possible to the human breast" agitated her during those first weeks of the work at Kamiah, as she caught an inside view of the difficulties of the progressive Indian and saw how the better part of the tribe was held down by the worst.

"Why don't these young fellows stand up and defy their oppressors? They would be strong enough if they would join hands and pull together."

"You have not taken into consideration that the whole might of the Government is back of the obstructionists," said the philosophic photographer. "The old chiefs die hard. They are intriguers and as two faced as white politicians. They are mischief makers and petty tyrants, as every man is tempted to be when in the possession of a little power. They have ingratiated themselves with Government officials and are made judges and police men." "If we resent their interference in our affairs," said an Indian to me yesterday, "we may be represented as insubordinates. We don't know; they come to us in the capacity of officers of the Government and what can we do?" "That's true," said Briggs, "The worst men in the tribe are the shrewdest politicians; they have the ear of the powers that be. Besides, the Agents sent to manage Indians often have a fear of them as a body and make use of the old chiefs as tools to control the others."

"Why," asked the Cook, "are not some of these Christian Indians put in places of trust?"

"Oh, you know that good Indians never give any trouble; they never need to be placated. The Agency is run on the principle of making the worst boy in school the monitor."

"And so," said the Cook, "as the goods issued to the tribe are distributed by the advice of these trusted men, I understand now why good Indians are still hauling their crops on raw hides, while wagons are falling to pieces on the land of the shiftless and worthless, never having had horses put to them since the day they were sent to their camp. I see why industrious men's farms are unfenced while rolls of wire lie rusting on the land of the favorites and relatives of these influential men of the tribe. If people outside really could see and understand how the Agency system works!". . .

Letter Eight

KAMIAH, CAMP McBETH
September 1st, 1889

It is refreshing to hear of you in New England enjoying a deluge while we are literally in danger of being burned up. You have read of our forest fires? perhaps in a half inch paragraph of the Journal, but you should hear the Photographer do justice to the situation! . . .

It is more than a month since the gold seekers in the mountains "let out" their camp fire, and the rainy season is not yet so close at hand as to give that prospect of relief which can be patiently waited for.

At night the sky is of a dusky red hue and now and then upon the hills a blaze spurts up like a beacon light and we know that the fire is creeping nearer and nearer. We have had no shower, since that which ushered us into this valley and there is no moisture any where, save in the little trickle of the diminishing spring from which we draw our daily supply, and in the more distant Clearwater River which moves along apprehensively in the copper-colored sunlight. . . .

We are still skirmishing on the outposts of our undertaking, still fighting preliminary battles and working on the collateral lines of our special object, Her Majesty bringing all her tact into play to overcome threatening obstacles, which, to one less conversant with Indian life and character, might prove to be insurmountable, and in the multiplicity and diversity of our cares, the days move rapidly, crowding each other off the scene.

The Special Agent has set up a blackboard in the office. It is the blackboard used long ago by the Missionary and, over the ghostly substratum of gospel texts, lessons in elementary surveying are given and sections are drawn and quartered and driven like wedges into the Indian brain by the Interpreter.

The Surveyor runs out the valley and makes straight the crooked ways of Paradise, while Her Majesty sits all day long in her inquisitorial chair (which is a wooden bench) solicitous of the uncles, aunts and cousins, tracing relationships through labyrinthian channels, searching after the suppositious head of the family who is to have 160 acres thrust upon him *nolens volens* when found.

This work of registry may seem to you an easy one to accomplish. That is because you do not know the intricacies of Indian relationships, nor the peculiarities of Indian custom and etiquette.

Indians come to the office to be registered as a necessary preliminary to allotment. Does Her Majesty say to the man or woman, "What is your name?" She knows better than that; such a direct method would not only fail to produce the desired result, but would insult the man, who must not speak his own name nor utter that of his wife. It may happen that he does not even know his wife's name, for Indians are addressed only by terms of relationship. To arrive at an Indian's personal name is a triumph of diplomacy. The name is sacred, not to be lightly spoken; you will understand that there is no question here of those appellations indiscriminately bestowed upon the unsuspecting savage by his guardians, the Agent, the Schoolmaster or the military man in charge of the nearest post. "Jack Ketch," "Holy Moses," "Bill Sykes," "Mary Mullony," "Lydia Pinkham," "Bob Sawyer" and "Yankee Doodle" are white men's jokes to the Indian and do not affect the integrity of his real name, which is cherished in a secure "secrecy," and which the white man seldom comes at in its purity, an illiterate interpreter's translation being the nearest approach. . . .

But, having at length obtained the name of the Indian before her, Her Majesty is encouraged to go upon the collateral lines. Here confusion is worse confounded. She must have the grandparents, as well as the aunts and uncles and children of the applicants for allotment, that, by means of cross references in her register, every person can be traced throughout the ramifications of the tribe to the remotest kindred. Now that the Indian is to own land in fee simple, the line of inheritance must be established.

But, when the Allotting Agent inquires for the grandparents, she is told that "all our father's uncles are our grandfathers and our mother's aunts are our grandmothers."

If she asks for the uncles, she is told that the mother's brother and the father's sister are uncle and aunt, but that the father's brother is also father and the mother's sister, a mother. Do you begin to see that the simplest case of registering a man and his wife is not, after all, so simple? You will be sure of it when you find that each Indian may have a dozen grandparents, as many more fathers and mothers, saying nothing of uncles and aunts and children.

To translate Indian relationships into English is a science by itself; do you wonder that the work of allotment is so long in getting started?

But the ponderous machinery has begun to move, though it does not yet run smoothly; there are unexpected frictions and breakdowns even in the department presided over by the Cook and Briggs finds use for all his good nature.

The men who have had the courage to volunteer as chainmen are not used to hard work. They can ride ponies all day but walking is a new sensation, their leg muscles are flabby and the sharp stones cut moccasined feet and so Her Majesty sends them to Mt. Idaho for hobnailed shoes.

The Nez Perces are not robust. Briggs weighs 260 lbs. and has the muscle of a prize Vermonter. Hobnailed shoes are a bagatelle to the Surveyor; they are impedimenta to the chainmen. They become wedged between the rocks and anchored in the bottom of the gulches. The poor fellows succumb crossing a cañon of only half pitch and they faint on the mountains with the thermometer at only 110° in the shade. They give out in the middle of the run, leaving Briggs to come home alone carrying the chain and shouldering his theodolite, ire in his footfall as he comes up the steps. At such times the Cook keeps out of his way unless she happens to have a mitigating tidbit in the pantry, which alas! is not often. Then the Special Agent hunts up a new crew; that is, she starts out in the search, but as she has no inducements to offer, money being no object to the Indian in general, one may imagine her success. But for the "returned students," that much-maligned class of Indians on the reservation, she must have gone outside the line and drawn her quota from the bordermen.

The new crew lasts a week or two; Briggs is an early bird and he wants to set out on his work just as the sun peeps over the hills upon the camp; but the Indians are not the early worms to come out at the call of the early-bird, they are not worms at all in this sense. They have not been used to responding to any call upon them and so Briggs wears out his tin pans playing reveille to little purpose. It would take a charge of dynamite to rouse the boys in time to suit the Surveyor. Indians have not learned to measure by the clock and they charge just the same to freight goods over a route four days long as over one they can make in a day. The element of time has not yet entered into their calculation, they estimate by the number of ponies required. Nor have they yet learned in any great measure the art of forecasting and often, just as the Surveyor is starting out on a new survey with his plans all made for a run of a couple of weeks, he is waited upon by Tom, Dick and Harry, with the information that they are out of grub. (Grub is Idaho for provisions.) The nearest depot of supplies is twenty-five miles distant, a two-days' journey with pack-saddles over the mountains, and the boys had waited to eat the last mouthful before thinking where the next would come from.

Then, to fill another gap in their education, Her Majesty has undertaken to teach the chainmen the ethics of partnerships in general and the arithmetic of their special combination. Hitherto, one man had brought a sack of provisions and all had fared sumptuously until the sack was empty. Then another man had brought a sack and the process was repeated; there had been no attempt at equalization; the sack of potatoes was just a sack and so was the sack of bacon or flour, or dried apples. Informed by the ubiquitous Cook of the irregularities in the chainmen's commissary department, Her Majesty appeared one morning at the boys' camp with four little blank books in her hand and took an account of stock. It was not easy to get at the facts; it was as difficult as to audit a county treasurer's books. She soon found that her plan could not be retroactive: she had to start anew. If Tom had put in twice as much as Dick, it was too late to remedy that. Dick could not see that he was any loser nor did Tom complain; he had eaten just as much and Harry also was content. It was his turn to bring the next sack and then it would be all right; it was all in the tribe anyhow and there would never be any trouble.

But the Special Agent gave each chainman a little book and showed him how to keep his account of all the money he expended for the general good and at the end of the month she said there must be a settlement and she would show them how that should be done. Then she inquired as to the diet of the men and disapproved of canned currant jelly as of a suspicious quality and of *pate-de-fois-gras* on account of its expense, and ended by sending Harry to Mt. Idaho to buy provisions, giving him a list of such things as were best for health and strength. . . .

But, in spite of obstacles, the work goes on steadily. To be sure, the Indians often destroy the Surveyor's corners as soon as his back is turned and make corners of their own. They are not so much to blame in this as would at first appear, for in the partial allotment of 1867, the Government put up fences to enclose each man's land, and the contractor ran his miserable apology for a fence, quite regardless of "lines," and enclosed plots of all sizes and shapes, quite oblivious to the points of the compass; and now the people say, "How is it? The Government made my fence; you say it is all wrong. Are there two Governments? and which is right? We will keep the land as it is; by and by another Government will come along and pull up our fences again."

Over and over the Surveyor marks the bounds until even

his patience is exhausted and he says to the Indians, "I will come back no more! Now, if you want to find your corners, you must send to Lewiston and pay another surveyor fifteen dollars a day to look for them."

* * *

It is two months since we left Lapwai and its turmoil far behind. What is happening at the Agency we have no means of knowing; our Interpreter, however, tells us that the appointment of the obnoxious Agent has been cancelled and a new man from Moscow chosen. James Reuben came back from Washington in due time and appeared at our camp, asking to be allotted. The prying Cook said he did not appear elated at the success of his mission and it was her opinion that the Nez Perces have "changed the name and kept the pain." The reputation of the man talked of as the next Agent is well known here; he is a political appointment under the Home Rule policy.[14]

Among the newspapers James brought was one from Portland, giving us the information that the Lapwai Indians were rising and that troops had been ordered to the neighborhood. This outside information of inside affairs was interesting to us, who were resting, so quiet and secure in our unguarded camp, with the Indians coming and going in their noiseless fashion and evidently becoming more and more friendly as the days pass by.

Letter Nine

KAMIAH
September 6th, 1889

This letter is to chronicle what Her Majesty calls "a bit of history." Her appellation is a relief to us; there is such irrevocableness, such predestination about it, which, on the con-

Alice Fletcher in the wagon in which she traveled about the reservation *(Idaho Historical Society)*

"Harriet"—Harriet Stuart—and her sister Annie Parnell Little *(Idaho Historical Society)*

First meeting to discuss allotment, at the First Presbyterian Church, Kamiah. Alice Fletcher at left (*Idaho Historical Society*)

Nez Perce mothers and babies (Idaho Historical Society)

"Bears' Paws Mountain"

Surveying: Alice Fletcher with her plat book at left (*Schlesinger Library, Radcliffe College*)

"They donned war bonnets." Young Nez Perce men pose for Jane Gay. (*Idaho Historical Society*)

trary, a bit of personal experience does not carry. We are not responsible for history; nobody is.

One hot Sunday, some four weeks ago, it was read out in church after the service, that in the morning, we would start for Cold Spring, about half way to Lapwai, where many of the Kamians had expressed a desire to be allotted.

Her Majesty read the list of names and impressed upon the men the importance of meeting her promptly, and on the morrow we packed our camp belongings and climbed out of the valley.

We pitched our tent at nightfall where there was a mud-hole and a clump of thorn bushes, and the following day we reached our destination and set up our housekeeping. We had provisions for six days and in that time we were sure to allot at least three-score Indians. We were very sanguine and we settled ourselves in that camp at Cold Spring with great expectations of much to come of it. . . .

We eat breakfast, sitting on the yellow grass beside the tinkling brook. Her Majesty is perched upon the box which carries the plats and Government papers, the Cook upon an upside-down horse bucket. The hens come to pick up the crumbs and this is the morning of the third day that we have been waiting for our Indians.

We have become inured to waiting, we have learned that it is not pleasant to an Indian to be hurried.

"You may chirrup to a horse," said the Cook, "but if you try it on an Indian, he stands stock still. If you keep on trying, he goes away in the opposite direction; his dignity is insulted." I sympathize with the workings of the Indian mind, for, if some gigantic philosopher should attempt to drive me out of my native sphere, to the planet Mars, for instance, I dare say I should pursue a line of action parallel to that of the Indian. I should want to think about it a good while. We are trying to drag and push and coax the aboriginal man into a new world and we really ought not to have been surprised that he kept us waiting three weeks at Cold Spring, in that hope deferred that maketh the heart sick.

A few white men came upon the scene the fourth day. They were "squaw men," rough, good-tempered, friendly fellows, who came to select land for their wives and children and in their wake came a few Indians from Lapwai. We were on the direct trail and Her Majesty stopped every one that was passing, took his registry and set him a work to find his allotment. . . .

In this way a week passes, then another, the Surveyor running out land farther and farther from the camp, until at length Her Majesty, the Cook and Photographer and James and the hens are left to the solitude of their own reflections, and still the Kamians came not.

Our provisions gave out one by one until we were reduced to the last pound of beef, the last ounce of sugar, flour and coffee. A white man, hunting cattle on the reservation gave us a half-dozen potatoes and we waited patiently while they lasted. Then an old miner from the gold placers of Elk City camped a little below us and the Cook went down to buy what he could spare. He had nothing to sell but he emptied his sack upon the ground and bade her take what there was. "I shall be in Lewiston tomorrow night or the day after," said he, "Me and my dog can get along till then."

There was enough to last one more day and the Cook took it, knowing that the man and the dog would go twenty-four hours on the strength of the supper then sizzling on the camp fire. Before the old man left us Her Majesty gave him a message to Briggs whom he would meet on his way.

"Tell him," said she, "that we are out of food and he must send us some at once." "And if I do not meet him," said the miner, "I'll send you some myself," and he mounted his pony and his pack horse and dog trotted after him out of our sight. . . .

That night a party of Lapwai Indians camped near us. They had ridden sixty miles to find the Allotting Agent that they might consult with her about their land which they were now ready to take. They were jolly young fellows who sang and told stories about the camp-fire and those among them who were "returned students" spoke good English.

Learning the perplexities of the Cook, they went out at daybreak with their shot guns and, on rising, we found a brace of grouse laid at the tent door. We learned some time after that the whole party had themselves subsisted on one bird and absolutely nothing else for twenty-four hours.

They had not been as fortunate in hunting as they had expected and had brought nothing with them but their powder and shot. They did their best to make our weary waiting endurable; they donned war bonnets and posed for the Photographer; they shot owls for the exercise of the Cook's taxidermist skill, and at last, tired of low rations, they formed in line and bade us an affectionate farewell out of a ghostly atmosphere of smoke into the recesses of which they rode cheerfully away.

Still we stayed on in hopes of hearing from Briggs and the Kamians, and . . . [finally] Briggs appeared upon the scene and dumped his well-filled saddle-bags at our feet.

The old miner had given our message and a freighter *had* been sent to our relief, who passed our camp and made no sign. Our driver had even inquired of the man and had been told there was nothing for us. "And his wife was sitting beside him when he said it," added James. Whether, in the mind of our driver, the heinousness of the freighter's conduct was increased or mitigated by the presence of his wife, was a question we did not stop to consider, for now a half-breed on his way from Kamiah to Lapwai tells us that the Indians we are waiting for had gone to the mines and would not be back for two or three weeks.

The Special Agent was silent upon the receipt of this information. She is not in a judicial frame of mind and she refrains from expressing an opinion lest she be unjust to the Indians. They had a chance to earn a few dollars, a chance which came rarely, in freighting supplies to the Chinamen at work in the mines. They could choose their land at another time. She tried to put herself in their place, but the Cook was not so considerate. . . . We packed our empty camp chest into the wagon, tied the hens on behind the seat, pulled up the tent stakes and started back over the trail to Kamiah. . . .

Letter Ten

. . . The results of our first organized campaign were not exhilarating and even Her Majesty who contrives to extract comfort from the most untoward circumstances, has preserved an expressive silence upon this part of our career.

We went out from Kamiah as lighthearted as the Federal troops when they crossed the Potomac on the 21st of May, 1861, and we also came back from our Bull Run with a healthy realization of the magnitude of the task we had undertaken.

But we were in nowise discouraged, for we could see that we were gaining the confidence of the Indians. Old Billy, the exponent of the Christian Kamians, came often to talk with us about Lewis and Clark and the exploits of his own grandfather and we had a speaking acquaintance with a good many shy men and women. They came many miles on their ponies to be registered and to ask advice about their allotments and we made the discovery that the women are more amenable to reason than the men; that they grasp a new idea more quickly and hold it more tenaciously and that when they make an appointment they generally keep it.

The Special Agent worked vigorously upon her register, the Photographer exploited the valley from one end to the other and Briggs hunted up the Kamiah widows and marked out their little garden plots and was pleased that they did not destroy his corner monuments but defended them from encroachment.

But the supply of Nez Perce widows was limited and could not keep us very long in the valley and now that the Lapwai Indians who went to Washington for Her Majesty's credentials had returned and the cordiality between the tribe and the Allotting Agent was on a firmer basis, one fine morning she notified the Cook of her intention to move camp upon the high ground where there were already some settlements along the streams and where the Surveyor had already begun his work. We would be gone several weeks, for there were many Indians who had promised to meet us and have their land surveyed and we must carry our whole camp outfit over the worst trails that ever civilized man trod. . . .

We pushed our way through a box cañon which led out from the valley, walking a great part of the way to ease the burdened horses, and arrived at the top having had good luck with only a few bits of harness broken and minus half a dozen bolts jolted from the wagon, the monkey-wrench, left on the ground after greasing the wheels, and a couple of shoes torn from Dick's fore feet in the rocky bed of the stream.

We pitched our tent on the side of a hill, near a hole in the ground at the roots of a tree.

In the hole was a little spring of water protected from wild cattle by a fence of logs. The Special Agent unpacks her plats, her inkstand and pen and is ready for business and she waits for her Indians. She waits all day and all night and then Briggs comes and pitches his tent and waits all day and all night. Then he runs out the land in the vicinity and finds the corners for three or four Indians who have made their selections and Her Majesty settles the disputes of a couple more and waits for the Kamiah men.

At the end of the fourth day, as the sun went down, a long haired Indian on his way to Mt. Idaho told us that he thought the men who were coming up to take land had all gone off that very day to the mountains to kill deer and would not be back for three months.

The Special Agent retires to the privacy of her tent to digest this information. Through the entrance-way she sees Briggs lying back against his saddlebags at the camp-fire. He is gazing up at the stars which are strangely dim, though it is a cloudless night. There is an unwonted look of anxiety upon his sun-browned face as he lays his pipe carefully down on a hummock of dried earth, and rises, and walks back and forth and looks east and west and north and south. The Cook, who is arranging her refrigerators for the night; hanging up various tin buckets on the high branches of the hawthorn trees, out of reach of the coyotes and dogs,—notices the Surveyor and, always inquisitive in the presence of a mystery, calls out,

"What is the matter?"

"Don't you smell the smoke more than usual?" Briggs replies.

"Yes, and see it also."

"The forest fires are spreading fast; it is bad for us."

"Why?"

"I cannot use the compass in Idaho; the needle hugs the earth; too much mineral, and don't you see I must have the sun to work by?"

"But the smoke can hardly put out the sun," says the Photographer, who also has an interest in that orb of day.

"Wait," says Briggs, "Wait and see and while you wait, pray for rain." . . .

Her Majesty lay down that night upon her stack of straw with a new anxiety for a pillow, and the Cook waked her at daybreak with the impertinent remark that "The King of France, with forty thousand men, marched up the hill and then marched down again." Briggs was frying his bacon and potatoes to the cheerful refrain of "John Brown's body lies a-mouldering in the grave," and Her Majesty hears the horses munching their barley near by. As her senses wake one by one, she is conscious of strong pine smoke, and that the atmosphere is blue and the sun very large, and it does not hurt her eyes though she looks it full in the face from the door of the tent. She hears Briggs say it is time for him "to be off; it is going to be a hot day" and when she emerges from the tent, it is just in time to see the surveying party against the sky as they pass over the hill, going to run out some land that he knows will be wanted by the recreant Kamiah men.

An hour later an Indian dashes into camp, inquiring for James the Interpreter. James' Mother is very ill and has sent for him. The hard-hearted Cook says, "James cannot be spared," which was true enough. "We expect," said she, "a large party of Indians to come at any moment and who will interpret for them?"

Her Majesty could not deny the expectation; every man who passed our camp on his way to or from Mt. Idaho knew that we were waiting for Indians and felt sorry for us. But James went, and the messenger remained in his place. He could speak a little English, and as for the horses, they could take care of themselves; they generally did.

James was gone two days and then returned with all his family's trials on his back, "sighing into everything he did." Then a summons came from Briggs to Her Majesty. It was a Macedonian cry "Come over and help." "The Indians are quarrelling about the land; come over and read the law to them." So the horses are put to the wagon and pull out, leaving the Cook to take care of the camp. She had put up a little lunch for the Special Agent and laid it carefully under the wagon seat and told her six times where to find it; then, feeling sure it would not even be looked for, she confided its whereabouts to the driver, and now stands at the door looking after the wagon as it winds slowly over the trail. She notices that Dick puts his feet down rather reluctantly, but this was his usual way of meeting any unexpected requirement. She watches until they pass over the hill and are lost to sight and then, taking the latest magazine, she sits down at the root of a tree and watches the camp with one eye while she takes in the "Century" with the other. . . .

* * *

At dusk, the wagon appeared over the hilltop, but Dick was no longer in the traces. At the end of the first mile he had fallen lame and, evidently in pain, refused to go farther. The crack in his hoof had developed into "the crack of doom"; it had reached the quick.

The Allotting Agent was forced to leave him with a white settler on the road and send to Briggs for one of his horses. When finally she joined the Surveyor, she found him worried by the espionage and interference of the white men on the border of the reservation near which he was at work. They follow him, offering advice, and intimating that they have rights which it would be well to respect; that it is folly to give the best land to the Indians, who would be just as well pleased to be left "in the cañons where they belong." They tell him that the people in an adjoining town have held an indignation meeting to discuss Her Majesty and to express their dissatisfaction with her methods; that they are going to ask their territorial delegate to insist upon her withdrawal and the substitution of a special agent who will do justice to the citizens.

One of these indignant citizens had a special indictment to lay before the meeting. He said that Her Majesty had been heard to call the attitude of the white people that of "buzzards sitting on a fence, waiting for the old horse to die." . . .

When she came up, she saw half a dozen of those border men hovering about, watching the grading of the land and near by stood the helpless Indians looking to her for what is their last chance in life though they may not realize it. Her eyes wandered from the red to the white man and back again to the ground on which she stood, gnawed down and trampled into barrenness by the white man's stock; she saw on the hills the Indian cattle lean and hungry, bound to starve if the rains do not come early enough to start the new growth of grass, and there waited the patient, cowed, hard-pressed little group, with eyes fixed upon her in what little faith remains in their race. Their clothes are mean, their faces have the dumb, pleading look so hard to bear the sight of; and as she gazes, the group takes in another form and face. They also are God's children and beside them stands the Elder Brother.

The surveyor is directed to run out the best land that can be found and the Indians are shown their boundaries in the presence of the greedy "actual settler" be he Irish, Dutch, Scandinavian, or born in Boston.

So far, Her Majesty has ridden about forty miles to each man she has allotted. If this is to continue and she lives to complete the two thousand allotments of the tribe, there will appear in the streets of Washington, in the century to come, a ghostlike form, twin sister to the Wandering Jew, staggering under the weight of her final report and asking of the astonished inhabitants for the long-ago-forgotten Indian Bureau.

The morning after Her Majesty returned to camp, with Briggs' horse in Dick's place, the mail arrived from Mt. Idaho and in it was an urgent request from the Department for a report of the exact number of Indians allotted each week.

Letter Eleven

CAMP CORBETT
October 16, 1889

Another day's journey brought us to our destined stopping place, and then we were just six miles, as the crow flies, from our last camp. We pitched our tent upon the land of Paul Corbett, an uncle of our driver and interpreter. He had enclosed with a rail fence a bit of "plow land" where there was a magnificent fir tree growing. James told us that we were now on one of the battle grounds of the Joseph war.

Paul courteously invited us to come inside the fence to be better protected from "stock," wild horses, cattle and pigs, all of which are commoners in Idaho.

Now, to be inside a rail fence was a desideratum. We had not sighed for a rail fence at Grizzly Bear Camp for it would have been no barrier to a bear. There is a satisfaction in braving a danger as big as a grizzly while there is no credit to be gained in defying pigs, and if there was any alleviation of pigs to be had, we were willing to take it. So, under the pressure of this one idea, we pitched our tent in Paul's plowed field, under the last and hottest September sun. . . .

The driver dug the usual trench fireplace and stretched

the wagon tarpaulin over it and the Cook set up her kitchen and all went merry as a marriage bell for a whole week. . . .

The Special Agent held court each day at the tent door, while, sitting on dried hummocks of plowed ground, rival claimants of land pled their cause. Sometimes it is a widow who comes to tell her story; standing her baby on its board against a tree or holding it on her knee, she fixes her wide-open eyes on the judge and tells how her land has been "jumped."

Then, perhaps half-a-dozen men have picked out the same 160 acres, and they come to the "Measuring Woman" for her decision of the knotty case. One had cleaned out the spring to establish his claim, one had hauled some rails, one had planted a stake or built a pile of stones or told some other Indian of his choice. They argue long and loudly and gesticulate violently and it looks as if a fight were imminent; but the moment Her Majesty decides who has the first right there is no more controversy.

There is no appeal and the contestants sit down together, divide their lunch, and go away satisfied.

Often there are disputes about boundary lines for the Surveyor's chain may cut a man's land in two, giving one half to the right hand neighbor and taking as much from the left and so three Indians are disgruntled and all three come to complain.

Then the Surveyor has to speak his little speech which he has learned by heart. "The lines must go East and West and North and South and all crooked fences must be made straight."

One shrewd old fellow says, "I want the Surveyor to *begin* at *my* land," and it takes an hour or two to convince him that Briggs can't begin anywhere but must follow out the lines already drawn. They look upon Briggs as a magician ever since he ran out the boundary line of the Reservation. It was at one of our first camps, "Bearing Tree," when the lines of the original treaty survey were being retraced. Many Indians had followed him through curiosity and one day he said, "There is a tree over there that has marks on it." It was a large pine tree and the Indians looked all over the trunk and found nothing.

Briggs said, "It is the bearing tree and has "N.P.R." [Nez Perce Reservation] cut on it." The Indians looked again and felt all over the rough bark. It was unbroken, no mark there.

Briggs came and with his hatchet laid bare a place about three inches deep and there, sure enough, were the letters "N.P.R."

"Now count the rings on the chips," said he. "You will find nineteen. It was nineteen years ago that the survey was made." This was enough for the Indians; they had implicit faith in the Surveyor after that. "He can do what he likes," they said.

One day a jolly old man with long hair and smooth face like an overgrown baby, with a dimple in each cheek and a twinkle in his eye, said to Briggs, after he had gone straight to a corner which the Indians thought they had so obliterated that it was impossible it should ever be found,

"Now I want you to find my Father."

"Where is your Father?"

"He is dead."

"All right," said the Surveyor, "but if I find him, you will have to take care of him, and, in the happy hunting ground, beef runs right into your mouth. Better go and see your Father." . . .

It is quite common, now, for the Indians to ask the Surveyor's advice about their allotments and that is a great step forward. Sometimes one will say, "I want *this* land." "Not if I can help it," says Briggs "You'll starve to death on that land; sage brush wont grow on it."

"This is my land," says another.

"Do you want to set up a rattlesnake farm?" says Briggs. . . . And the Indians laugh and, in nine cases out of ten, take his advice. The tenth comes back, after his poor land is run out, and with shamefacedness says

"I got bad land, all alkali, no good for grain, no good for nothing: what I do now?"

"Guess you'll have to marry that woman who picked out

that splendid piece of land yesterday. It is worth twenty dollars an acre today," says Briggs solemnly.

"That woman married already," says the man.

"Oh, then you'll have to eat alkali."

But the man persists. He has found a good farm with a spring on it that nobody has chosen.

"You don't know what good land is. Where is it? Well! I'll look at it. You go and see the Special Agent. She has no time to bother with such fellows as you, but you can go and try." And so the man comes to camp and tells his tale of woe and goes away comforted with a bit of paper in his hand for Briggs.

Camp Corbett is within a dozen miles of the border of the Reservation along which many white men have settled on small farms. Some of them have married Indian women and they come to us to have their children allotted.

They are rough enough, most of them; some are stranded men of innate refinement; others old college men who came West in '49 and "lost their grip," wandered out into the wilderness and took up a claim. It is pitiful to see them; the look of surprised memory that comes into their faces as they meet Her Majesty: the breaking open of the rough crust, and the softened tone, and the better English that rises to the surface; the little polite ways that creep shyly back. Perhaps they are beguiled into speaking of a past they have tried hard to forget but which the voice of Her Majesty has vividly recalled.

One who came out just from college had a brother who was a doctor or a lawyer in the East and he says, "They have lost sight of me and believe me dead."

"Do you ever think of going back to your friends?"

"Oh, no, but I want my children educated." . . .

The Indians respect this class of white men and they live in amity and help each other, but there are other settlers along the line that over-reach the Indian in all possible ways. They drive sharp bargains with him, they encroach upon his land: they push their fences out upon it and let down the bars and turn large herds of cattle out to eat and tramp his grass.

They put their own brand on the increase of his cattle, coming on the Reservation Sunday, when they know the owner will be at church. They gather up the "slick ears" (un-branded calves) and boldly put their own brand over that of the Indian as if they had bought the animal. . . .

These border men have been very civil to us. They have things to sell and we buy cabbages and poultry at "market rates." As we have no way of getting at quotations of Idaho produce prices, we trust the border men with the absolute faith of his Indian neighbor and he sells us his biggest and oldest hens for all they will weigh, considerately charging no extra for age or experience. . . .

One day . . . an Indian galloped up with a message to the effect that the Superintendent of Indian Education had come from Lapwai to Kamiah to see the Special Agent, could she come down? . . .

At daylight, we were on our way to Kamiah, taking with us a loaf of bread and our hen. The other had disappeared in the night. We arrived as the people were going into the church for it was Sunday. Her Majesty dismounted and met the Superintendent inside, the Interpreter remained on duty, and the Cook retired to our cabin. . . .

* * *

We returned to Camp Corbett Sunday night and as we came out upon the high ground, a black cloud gathered over our heads and the driver said we must run, but neither the lay of the land nor our horses were adapted to running.

There was no road, only a pony trail, and the storm caught us before we could gain the shelter of our tent. We spread our waterproofs over the government papers, which, for safety, had always to be with us, and took the rain full in our faces until at last, damp and cold, we scrambled under the canvas; Home, sweet home! Yes! a tent in a plowed field in a storm of wind and rain. Not quite satisfying, perhaps, but we actually felt a sense of comfort stealing over us as we sat on pack saddles and boxes around our fourteen inch sheet iron stove and felt the drops patter on the cloth and sizzle on the stove pipe, splash over the camp bed and leak through the thin places of the canvas, down upon our backs. . . .

We enjoyed the rain all the next day, for it was more than four months since a drop had fallen. But it kept on, and the

71

stain of the black soil creeps higher and higher up our tent and James drives its pegs more firmly into the water soaked earth and the drops beat through the sloping side of the canvas in a fine spray. The Cook puts the Photographer's camera under the bed and goes out in waterproof and rubber shoes to coax a little smoke out of the pine chips but has to give up the idea of anything hot for dinner.

On the third day, we are fatigued with our exertions trying to keep dry. We cannot put any energy into our hopeless task and we begin to find excuses for the Indian's inertia. We sit down ourselves now and take it as it comes. The rain falls through the tent opening down upon our bed and makes pools on the rubber blanket; the stove, kept at full blast, sends up great flakes of lampblack, product of the combustion of pitch pine, which fall back like infernal snow upon our heads. It adheres to our papers and smutches our clothing, our tent is stained inside and out and its floor trampled like a cattle pen. We have fresh straw spread but are conscious of the substratum and, at the end of a week, we are horrified when we look at each other. . . .

In the morning the rain has ceased and the Cook calls the Special Agent to her tent door to look at the sky. Great masses of broken clouds rush across a background of infinite blue and down in the valley where Kamiah lies, a snow white fog is in motion like a tumultuous sea. The mountains rise dark against the horizon and the enraptured Cook stands looking up into the parted heavens happily oblivious of the frying pan in her hand. Suddenly, a blast drops down from some lofty frigid height, scoops up the fog from the valley and dashes it in her face. In the twinkling of an eye she is enveloped in a dense cloud. Shivering, and with teeth chattering, she finds her way into the tent, choking with the fog she cannot breathe. She is wet as by a shower and her fire is out, and hungry and chilled to the bone, we hug the tent stove and expatiate on the climate of Idaho.

In a quarter of an hour the restless Cook draws the flap of the tent and looks out. So! the sky is cloudless and miles deep, the horizon line sharp and there is not wind enough to stir a leaf. . . .

Now we dry our belongings in the sun. The tent is cleaned thoroughly, Her Majesty takes her office out of doors and we wait for the mud to dry up so that communication can again be established between our camp and that of the Surveyor. While we have been besieged by the elements, he has been sheltered only by a tarpaulin a few miles distant but to make those few miles there is a labyrinthine detour to go over. He is so near and yet so far. A message came from him yesterday that we ought to break camp at once and return to Kamiah: that at this time of year we were liable to have prolonged storms and nights too cold for tent life. So today we are gathering up our belongings. Pack horses will be here early in the morning to take our blankets at ten cents a pound and our grain at two cents. Not that a pound of bedding is heavier than a pound of barley, but it takes up more room and the Nez Perce way of estimating values is by the number of ponies required.

Old Billy has just passed our camp on his way to Genesee to fetch a silver service which has arrived from Washington by express, a gift to the Kamiah church, and we have sent him for a fur robe. As I write, rain begins to fall. We must hasten on.

* * *

Letter Twelve

KAMIAH
November 17, 1889

We shall probably do no more field work this season. We hurried down from Camp Corbett, for a storm which the Surveyor's barometer foretold would be severe was close upon us. We ran before it all the way and did not escape a wetting but, as we came out of the gulch into the valley, our little cabin lay hot in the sunlight and there was no sign of rainfall in all the cañon. On the uplands we had left not only the young grass had started but the color was creeping up in the old yellow stalks, a phenomenon new to us, though the Indians said it was always so after the Fall rains set in. The smoke in the valley was thinner but in a few days it grew dense again: the forest fires were not extinguished; they were not materially checked.

Old Billy came back with our furs and the precious communion service. He had taken his wagon over the mountain to fetch it, lest it be injured on a pack horse. He told us that the Kamians had to go to the mountains much earlier this year because the drought had burned their gardens and they had nothing to eat. They would all starve unless they killed much deer and caught much fish to dry for the winter's food. Billy says he is too old to hunt any more. Long ago he hunted much for "King George" (Hudson's Bay Co.) and he inconsequently added that "King George told Indians to get more wives so as to have more skins cured"; but it was not the Nez Perce way and Billy and his one wife have grown old together.

We were glad that the old man told us why the Kamians had disappointed us at Camp Kincaid; we were also glad of our own experience at Cold Spring. It is good to be pinched a little: it teaches charity towards those who are pinched a good deal. Her Majesty was opening the mail old Isaac had brought and she thought he looked hungry. After that every Indian looked hungry in our eyes. It takes a bit of personal experience sometimes to correct the angle of vision. . . .

We have bought another horse, George, the tallest of his species I ever saw and whose age is past finding out, but he will trot steadily all day with a heavy pack and never swerve an inch from the line and he pulls like a machine. He has no nerves to be guarded against and is altogether the most responsible member of our party.

We have use for all our means of locomotion for the season of out door work is passing rapidly. The forest fires still rage with new impetus and we watch at nightfall the tall columns of flame as the solitary pine trees on the hills are consumed by the all devouring element. It creeps nearer and nearer until it seizes upon the hay stacks of the Indians and our world is all yellow and burnt, while the smoke is so dense that it is high noon before the sun casts a faint blurred shadow. From twelve noon to three P.M. is all the time the Surveyor's instrument will work and at twenty rods distance one can scarcely tell a man from a tree. . . .

It was growing unpleasantly cold and we stepped out of our cabin every morning into a thick fog which wet us like an icy rain and our stock of fuel had given out. The resourceful Briggs set his men to chop down a dead tree which stood not far outside our fence.

The first blow of the axe brought old Mother Lawyer in a rage to the spot.[15] Fortunately she raged in the vernacular and the ideas she expressed so forcibly could only be guessed at for James seemed unwilling to interpret them in any degree of literalness. But it was evident that she claimed the tree as her personal property and was exasperated at us for daring to touch it.

Old Mrs. Lawyer has the reputation of being a *tewat*, or sorcerer, and the Nez Perces have not yet arrived at the stage of development characterized by scorn of the tewat's power; the farthest along would rather not excite their enmity.

The chainmen, axe in hand, stood as if petrified by fright; Briggs, leaning aginst the dead tree, white and scarred by sun and wind, was kicking with the toe of his shoe the little pile of chips and whistling soundlessly to himself while James, bare-headed, twirled his hat and looked irresolutely from the tewat to the Surveyor as we came upon the scene.

At our appearance there was a fresh excess of rage on the part of the tewat, emphasized by unmistakable gesticulation.

The Allotting Agent laid her hand on the arm of the old woman and looked in her face.

"What does she say, James? Tell her she must speak quietly."

"She says," said James, "that you have taken her tree."

75

Her Majesty kept hold of the woman's arm and the tewat quieted down: something she saw in the Allotting Agent's face made her drop her angry eyes.

"Tell her, James, that we did not know the tree was claimed by any one in particular. We were very cold and with the trees all about it is strange that the Indians should grudge us a little wood to keep us warm; what does she want us to do?"

"She says that she is poor and you are rich."

"Oh! she wants pay for the tree?"

"I think so," said James.

"Tell her it was not a nice way to come storming at us like a wild beast: we are willing to pay for everything we use," said the Cook. "It is a pity that Indians are so slow in developing the virtue of neighborly kindness." "Ah well," said Her Majesty, "Christian graces were long in growing upon our own race, and these poor things do not often see shining examples of disinterested benevolence."

"She says that she does not grudge you the tree *now*," said James, "and that if you will give her something when you go away, she will be satisfied."

Then we shook hands all around and the *tewat* was our fast friend from that day. But the old woman's tree could not keep us warm, for the boards of our cabin were full of wood-pecker's holes and draughts came in through a multitude of cracks. So long as it was light enough to be actively busy we did not suffer, but at nightfall we covered over the little box stove and tried to forget our misery in the perusal of "Mr. Barnes of New York" or the antique Missionary Heralds which constituted the library at our disposal. . . .

The sunflowers and goldenrod have gone to seed long ago and still half a dozen Kamiah Indians hold out and will not take their land.

Now Her Majesty would have stayed all winter in that cañon to catch those few Indians if the Cook would have staid and the provisions would have lasted but she was po-litely informed one day that there was no widow's cruse of oil or bag of meal in the pantry and if she contemplated a winter's sojourn in Paradise she must lath and plaster its walls and install a steam heating apparatus. Then there was a consultation with Briggs and a little expedition up the valley to say goodbye to the half-dozen Indians who were "holding out."

All up and down the valley we rode and whether the business air of our whole team impressed the aboriginal mind as to the futility of holding out, or whether the fear of the best land being allotted without their having a chance at it proved the means of saving repentance, at all events, the last man of them was registered and we rode home as if in a triumphal car.

Today the wagon is being repaired and the horses shod and when next you hear of us, we shall be miles and miles away from this haven of rest in the midst of a troubled land.

Letter Thirteen

HOME
December 26, 1889

The scene has changed as you will see by the date of this letter. We are no longer living a savage life. . . .

Our coming out of the valley of Kamiah was a matter of much more deliberation than our ingoing. We had to buy a third horse to put with one borrowed from the Surveyor so as to double our team, and we crawled up out of the great gulch as if leaving all we loved behind. We had been loath to start, for at the end of two days journey lay Lapwai with its unknown quantity of trouble waiting for us. We had heard of the appointment of a new agent to take the place of the obnoxious man, but we had also been told that the Lapwai Nez Perces were still arrayed in opposition to the allotment. . . .

At last, on the 16th of November, as we were coming

across the ferry from a visit to the old Chief Utzen Malli-can,[16] one of the most obstinate obstructionists, some subtle change in the atmosphere attracted our notice. It was Saturday. Her Majesty said, "We must start at once for Lapwai." "Impossible until Monday," replied the Cook, "Not an Indian would move hand or foot to help us on Sunday, and we must have pack horses to get out of this cañon."

No one disputed the Cook; we knew she was right, so we planned for Monday. . . .

That last night in Kamiah was very cold. We sat in great coats about the stove and listened to the ominous sounds in the chimney, but we did not talk much: each was thinking hard and fast. Each had a special work to do on the morrow and it must be well under way by daylight. Briggs would rise superior to the tardy November sun and the Cook,— well, the Cook always began to get her breakfasts the night before.

One by one we slipped away from the small circle of warmth about the stove and drew our two pairs of blankets around us. The black cat, sensible of something unusual in the air, crept upon the camp bed and snuggled down at the feet of Her Majesty. . . .

At daylight, the Cook gave him his breakfast; an enormous breakfast, much as one would give all the delicacies of the season to the man condemned to die before dinner time. As if she could feed that cat into unconsciousness of what was going on about him!

Our own breakfast was shortened for we were all in unwonted haste. Bags and bundles were rushed out into heaps in the yard, boxes nailed up and stored away in the cabin, windows made fast, the doors locked and the key given to Old Billy, who was on hand helping to lift and carry. Other friendly Indians came to see us off, hanging about in dumb interest, ready to pack the horses or stow away our belongings in the wagons and when we were in the midst of it all, Elder Felix drove up with his spring wagon and a pair of tough little mules.[17] He lifted various bundles, weighed them in his hand, examined the pack saddles, equalized the burdens and filled his own wagon with various boxes and packages.

"What are you doing, Felix?" said Her Majesty. "I go up the hill," said he. "I take something: too much load for you."

"That's good of Felix," said the Cook.

"Hill very bad," said Felix, "We start soon?" and he looked up at the sky anxiously. The Cook noticed that he had put an armful of wood in his wagon. She wondered, but was too busy to ask why he did it, and we drove out of the yard, Old Billy putting up the fence behind us. . . .

As we passed up the valley, an old woman came out of her tent to bid us good bye and as long as we were in her sight, she stood, arms raised and voice ringing out to the darkening sky. James told us she was invoking a farewell blessing upon us. "She is very old and thinks she may never see you again."

Notwithstanding the haste we had made, it was nearly noon when we began the ascent of the steep hill up which we had always walked to ease the horses. As Her Majesty stopped her team and dismounted, Felix jumped from his seat. "No! No!" he said. "My mules strong, I take you," and before the Special Agent could demur, she was in his light wagon and the mules going up at a brisk pace.

On reaching the high ground, we expected our Indian friend to bid us goodbye and turn back, but he said, "I camp tonight—camp pretty soon, dark before long you think?" and so it came about that Felix planned for us. He chose the camping place where there was a little water but no wood. Then he kindled us a fire from his armful in the wagon and we boiled our coffee and crept between our blankets wondering why Felix had come, and thinking if he had not come, how much less comfortable we would have been.

When we awoke at dawn, a little fire was blazing on the frozen ground outside, a bucket of water was at our tent door and the wagon all ready.

We were soon in motion, Felix still keeping on with us.

"I go to Lapwai," said he, "my wife she go with the children."

We overtook the wife and children trotting along on their ponies. They had started in advance.

The second day's journey brought us to Cold Spring. We had passed our old camping place and pitched our tent on the hill beyond for Felix said it was warmer among the trees on the high ground.

That night as we were preparing supper, shivering close to a blazing pine fire, Felix's little boy Paul brought us a two quart jar of fresh milk, a present from his father, who had brought it for us from Kamiah. Milk toast for supper and oat meal and milk for breakfast! Think of it! So fortified, what perils by the way could jostle our equilibrium? It was luxury unexpected. How we blessed Felix! . . .

It blew a gale that night and the rain dashed in sheets against our tent so violently that we got up and dressed and waited impatiently for day to break that we might hurry on before the rain-soaked earth would make the descent to Lapwai dangerous.

Everything has an end and so had this journey over the mountains for we slid down into the little valley in time to cook our supper under a roof. As we ate it, warm and dry beside the stove, we thought of Felix and his family, camped outside in his shelter tent on the wet earth, and not until we had seen them comfortably housed could we lie down to sleep the blessed sleep of the tired. When we woke, the snow covered mountains were glistening white in the sun. We had crossed none too soon. No more camp life for us this year. We tried it once again, going with Felix and his brothers to the north part of the Reservation to grade and survey a piece of land they had chosen, but when we reached the place, the little company of Indians were discouraged. The allotment of eighty acres of unbroken snow did not appeal to the enthusiastic side of their nature. They made haste to return to the sheltered cañons and after lodging over night at a settler's house, we also set our faces toward Lapwai. . . .

It was now the last of November and while the Cook went to Lewiston to arrange for our departure eastward, Her Majesty held a council with the Lapwai Indians who were still opposed to the allotment. The council was a stormy one and there were many angry denunciations and threats of violence. James said there were "knives under the blankets," and after the Council had broken up in a good deal of excitement, an old medicine man undertook the task of killing Her Majesty "with his eye." He, with several other Indians who were in the secret of his intentions, followed the Special Agent to her office where the "tewat" wrestled with his occult powers until Her Majesty, wishing to be alone, cleared the room and the old fellow, muttering in his impotent rage, strutted out to explain to his friends as best he could why he had failed. What ever his explanation may have been, the Indians came to the conclusion that "the Measuring Woman" was stronger than the sorcerer and a respect for her power began to appear among them.

After that we folded our tent, packed our camp equipage in boxes, left Briggs to finish up what surveying was practicable, and turned our longing eyes Eastward. . . .

Letter Fourteen

Lapwai
May 11th, 1890

We left Washington as the lilac buds were unbuttoning their winter coats and that noisy busybody, the English sparrow, had set about repairing his last season's nest in the ivy vine beneath my eastern window. We resolutely turned our backs upon the beauty of spring, the rest of the home circle and the comforts of right living, and we bought our tickets to the Nez Perce land, with a stop over privilege for Nebraska, as the Department wished Her Majesty to take in the Omaha and Winnebago by the way, to tie up some loose ends of their affairs.

It is two years since the allotment of the Winnebagoes,

and, though the majority of them have not been swift to see the beauties of the citizenship thus conferred upon them and have been slow to perceive the justice of the white man's law; and have raised, some of them, their small moccasined feet to kick against the iron shod inevitable, Her Majesty's eye of faith sees still their growth in grace. Though in her absence from them there have been many skips and tumbles in the tribe, a sort of kaleidoscopic shifting of the wives and husbands and children, to the detriment of the family grouping system of allotment, she wraps about these nascent citizens her ample robe of charity, woven so closely as to hide all but the spark of divinity that makes the whole world kin.

While she plans an amendment to the Severalty Act which shall give to every Indian his 80 acres, independently of his age, sex, or previous condition of marriage, she picks up the trailing virtue and splinters the broken spirit. She starts again in the right way the man who had lost his path, gives impetus to the halting and hope to the despondent. She will not despair of any! In her prophetic vision she sees her Indian friends as those who have already "come up out of much tribulation."

There were many complaints to listen to, many adjustments of difficulties to make: many appeals for help to be sorry for, for the Agency system has taught the man to seek aid from outside and not to stiffen up his own muscle and work out his own salvation. Government pabulum makes gelatine, not bony structure. Indian legs and arms, with the strong meat of enforced self-dependence, will stiffen in time, but bones do not harden in a day, and the transition period is not picturesque.

It is pitiful to see the dazed apprehension of the old Indian when forced to *think*, as he is being forced now by the necessity of self preservation: but it is encouraging to notice that the young are learning to forecast and prepare for the future. . . .

We went to the Omahas to help them. Her Majesty had in mind the people she had left struggling to comprehend the new conditions she had brought upon them. They were babes suddenly raised to their feet and told to walk and her heart had ached for years that she had not a thousand hands to hold out to them. She had at last an opportunity to give them a lift. A fund of some $10,000 had been diverted from the support of their school, (said school to be carried on out of the general appropriation), and this $10,000 would help many to get on their feet.

She went joyfully to the Omahas. I went also, with the pleasing picture in mind of a happy hen brooding a lot of helpless chickens, some of them with the bits of shell still sticking to their pin feathers. In the evening of the first day, I saw a disconsolate, puzzled hen. Her progeny were all ducks and had taken to the water. Do you comprehend? The Omahas are full fledged and, in some sort of way, are paddling themselves in their sea of trouble. It is too late to help them arbitrarily as one would help a nursing child. In the council Her Majesty called to explain her purpose, the first question asked was, "Where does this money come from?" Upon explaining that it was the interest upon the money paid the tribe for lands they had sold, they said: "Then it is ours: we will take it in cash, and spend it for ourselves. We are not children, we are citizens."

"But," said Her Majesty, "the law will not give it to you in cash." They replied that they did not understand what right any one had to make a law about their money without consulting them.

Then they were told that in reality this money was a gift, since the burden of their school had been taken off the tribe.

"It is unmanly to take gifts," said the Omahas.

"But this money is to help those of you who need assistance on your land." They replied, "It belongs to all." One said, "I should not like to think my land was ploughed with money belonging to women and children." Others said it was not fair: a per capita distribution was the only just way. And even the old and shiftless resented this paternal interference.

It would be hard to say whether Her Majesty was glad or sorry at the unexpected attitude of the Omahas. We had gone so far, on the presumption that the wards of the nation could have no will of their own, as to stop in Chicago and get estimates of the cost of small frame houses which the Government was willing to erect for the "most deserving," of course, and pay for out of the $10,000. We had also ascertained the price of wagons and harness and had been as pleased as if we had been buying Christmas gifts for a Charity Hospital. . . .

At last, the Photographer packed up his souvenirs, and, leaving the Omahas to the enjoyment of their pride, we ploughed our way through the black gumbo mud to the railroad station, and one day in the latter part of April, the little steamer "Annie Nixon" touched the wharf at Lewiston, and we had come back to the Nez Perces as we had gone from them, on the yellow Snake River.

Our thoughts had been busy all the way up. This time we knew what we were coming to, at least, we believed we knew: there was no charm of the unknown hanging over the Reservation: it lay all bare and bald before us and we felt no valor born of ignorance.

We set our teeth as close together as we could for the sand cloud which broke upon our boat as we touched the pier, and stepped out of our cabin with plenty of grit to begin with.

Our Interpreter met us on the gangway. He said he had "lots to tell," and then he lapsed into his normal melancholy. His "lots" has not yet all been told: it is articulated by spurts, under pressure, and the supply is apparently inexhaustible.

When we left the Reservation last December, the wind of its normal strife had shifted from the Agency quarter and the storm was centered over the school locality. Its officials were "all by the ears" more literally than could be imagined by sober people of the outside world, and now, on our return, the result was just being declared.

The dead and wounded were being removed from the field of battle. Victory had perched upon the banner of a fresh aspirant for the superintendency of the school and the old incumbent, still in charge, was waiting only to turn over Government property to his successor.

Her Majesty had applied for quarters in some one of the unoccupied Government buildings and we now drove up to the one assigned us. Harriet, the wife of our driver, stood in the doorway, and we noticed that, for an Indian, her face was somewhat elongated. At sight of us she burst out with, "We've done the best we could, but this house is a sore eyed hospital, and the front room is a dead house, and the bed they left for you had a girl die on it two days ago, and I threw the bed and blankets out of the window, but it is too bad."

"What *do* you mean?" said Her Majesty, as she slowly stepped down from the wagon. "Mr. Superintendent thinks you had something to do with his removal," said James, our driver, in a helpless tone of voice.

"Where is Mr. Superintendent?" asked the Cook.

"Sitting on his porch looking at us: he thinks he is happy," said Harriet, as she stepped aside and we entered the place.

With the exception of an iron bedstead and a cracked box stove which lay on its side in the front room, the house was absolutely empty. Harriet and James had procured the stove, but could do no more for our comfort, when all the resources of the locality were under the control of our amiable neighbor the waning autocrat. The walls were smeared and broken, the floors indescribable and the atmosphere stifling. . . .

"Very well," came at last from the Allotting Agent: it was her acceptance of the goods the gods did not provide. "All right," echoed the Cook. "We have three or four hours of day light yet. Hurry up, James, and unload the wagon, turn out the horses and then go over to the ware house and bring our camp bed and blankets." (We had packed them in boxes last winter when we left Idaho.)

"Oh, the box that had the bedding in it is broken open and empty. I was in the warehouse last week and saw that all your boxes had been ransacked," and James looked more and more depressed. "Well bring what there is left," and then, in the spirit of our forefathers, we set to work to achieve our independence. Before those three or four hours of daylight were gone, the house had been thoroughly washed with a solution of carbolic acid, (the resident physician had been compelled to supply disinfectants and deoderizers, the iron bedstead had followed the mattress out of the windows, the glass of which was no longer opaque; our own camp cot had been brought in; a sack filled with wheat stubble, upon which was spread our fur carriage robe, made the substratum of our couch, and two down pillows which a friend had put into the Cook's trunk in Washington, were placed in position and we smiled at the impotence of circumstances. . . .

The Idaho sun woke us at five o'clock, staring in so boldly as to reveal our surroundings in an uncomfortable vividness. . . .

No matter! Here is a new day, and we rise to meet it. Indians straggle in to look after their land. Reports are to be written, weekly and monthly and quarterly statements to be made. Surveys are to be gone over, quarrels to be settled, rival claims to be adjudicated. Behold Her Majesty, triumphant over the hardships of life, seated at the board table, like a queen on her throne, pen in hand, writing her decrees. . . . There she sits in aggravating persistency, listening to the stupid, advising the vicious, stiffening up the weak, forgetting to rest, studying how to help those who won't (she says, *can't*) help themselves; unmoved under abuse, steadfast under calumny.

It is enough to drive a looker-on to madness. There is not an Indian with hair so long and blanket so dirty but can claim her attention, be she ever so faint with hunger and the Cook ever so impatient. . . .

* * *

In a few weeks, we shall cross the mountains to Kamiah, the lovely valley of the Clearwater, to our little cabin, where the polecats under the floor await our coming, the magpies in the yard talk of us and the black cat, we hope, will come out to meet us. Kamiah will again be our base of operations.

In the meantime, there is much ploughing and harrowing and sowing of seed to be done here, in preparation for the time when we finally come back to the Lapwai Indians and their day of grace is past: when, like refractory sick children, they *must* take the medicine that is best for them. But we are longing for the camp and the pulls up and down the cañons, and the sunburns, the fierce appetites and the bark of the coyote in the still night; the tramp, tramp of the cattle on the hills and the woodpeckers making holes in the board side of our cabin, the noiseless coming and going of the moccasined Indians and the flitting shadows of the clouds upon the Clearwater as it gurgles through the valley. . . .

Letter Fifteen

KAMIAH, N.P.R.
June 24th, 1890

We arrived at Lapwai on the twenty-eighth of April and plunged at once into a sea of troubles—not our own, but, all the same, a hindrance to our work.

Added to the perennial quarrels of the officials, there had been worked up during our absence a strife among the Indians themselves; and their methods did not differ very much from the methods of border warfare among their white neighbors. The *casus belli* was the waning power of the old chiefs, who die hard and are belligerent to the last. It is a struggle of "Christianity against Heathendom," as the missionary expressed it; one might say—of civilization against barbarism: it means the same thing: it is the throes of evolution.

Among the Kamiah Indians, Robert Williams, pastor of the native Presbyterian church, has resisted almost single handed the baleful influence of the old chiefs and *tewats*, or sorcerers, of the tribe; the fight was now against him, and it was led by some of the shrewdest men of both Lapwai and Kamiah. They had managed, after exhausting their own peculiar style of persecution, to reinforce themselves with the aid of the Agent, and had quite skilfully gained the notice of the Presbytery of which Robert, as a minister, was a member.

Before this body of unsuspecting ministers they brought

charges of immorality and procured the evidence of an old woman who had cooked for Robert one day, in the absence of his wife, a year previous to his arraignment. The Presbytery appointed a commission to come upon the Reservation and try the case, and the whole tribe was rent in twain.

The trial was a sad farce, though not differing very much from official investigations in general and not so far removed from ordinary law processes out here in the border land of civilization. The testimony was all in the vernacular, the interpreter doubtful and the commission mistook the identity of the witnesses. The prosecuting Indians were skilful, some of them being astute enough to blind any set of well meaning men ignorant of the Indian's language and tactics.

There was a great inconsequential buzz and, in the midst of it all, stood Robert, calmly waiting the issue and thinking of Ham, who, when reviled, reviled not again.

At last the sentence came, in terms the Indians could not understand but misconstrued for the most part, misinterpreted as it was by the mischief makers. The commission found Robert not guilty of the charge, but guilty of imprudence, in that he had a woman to cook for him in the absence of his wife; and they suspended him for six months with loss of salary.

Some of us who had just come from the outer world, where it was not a sin to have a woman cook, were stirred up by this verdict; our Cook especially, being a woman of the most pronounced type and a Presbyterian of the bluest hue, took the matter to heart, and said disrespectful things about people passing judgment in cases where their ignorance was conspicuous.

As for Robert, he went home to Kamiah, and, as he could not preach in his own church, he took to mission work outside, and bided his time with a sweet and unresentful patience. Knowledge does not always strengthen faith. Here was Robert, who could not see beyond his little hour, *sure* that all things would work for good to him, for did he not love God, and *that was the promise*; and there were the two faithful missionaries, who looked far into the future and could trace cause to its unerring effect, staggered at the increase of power the outcome of this trial would throw upon the side of the old chiefs and tewats of the tribe as against the progressive and Christian Indians.

Miss Sue at Mt. Idaho has set herself to right the wrong and we know that she will do it. It does not seem to us a hard task: it has simply been a mistake such as is often made in matters where wisdom is more necessary than goodness and where compromise is resorted to.

A new Superintendent of the Government school at Lapwai was installed soon after our arrival; an Irishman, with a full blown brogue to recommend him. He came from Genesee one hot afternoon, on foot, carrying his coat on one shoulder and a small bundle, hanging from a stick, over the other. He proved to be a mild and harmless simpleton, who may have been, in his youth, tinctured with Thoreauan philosophy; at all events, he preferred to do his own cooking in his own little skillet in his own office, and to take his grog in a solitary unassisted way.

He carried his official correspondence in his coat pocket, to be handy and left the key to the Government warehouse in its lock for the same reason. When it became necessary to render a "monthly statement" he was as one walking in his sleep; there was not a fibre in him on which to hang a thread of responsibility. The school employees tried to help him, but as the cook said, "one might as well try to make a wet towel stand alone." The only educational effort he was ever known to make was when he attempted to teach some infant Indians to sing an Irish song.

He never arrived at the remotest conception of the duties of his office. He said, "A schule it was I came to keep and a sthore it is." I doubt not it was a consolation to the passing Superintendent, who was "a man of parts," but of the wrong politics, to foresee the state of affairs which would follow his own retirement. But the Irishman's term of office was brief and he made no resistance when he was removed. He borrowed money enough to take him off the Reservation, saying he would try to find something to do near by. We heard of him wandering about among the small towns for awhile before he was lost in the general wreckage of the far West;

and then something happened which astounded us all: the actual appointment of a right man to the right place. Mr. McConville was installed at Lapwai as Superintendent of the school and in twenty-four hours every Nez Perce knew and rejoiced thereat, and now we venture to hope that *all* the lions of the Reservation will not be rounded up and massed in *our* way, and that there may be, in some measure, that cooperation which the Department expects from its employees.

Her Majesty has been urging Mr. McConville to ask the Indian Department to allow the school a U.S. flag and instruments for a band: there are boys here who can be trained to play and young men, returned students, who can teach them.[18]

On Decoration Day we happened to see the procession of school children going out to decorate the graves of the soldiers who slew their fathers in the Joseph war. The graves lie outside the school grounds and near by are some smaller mounds of the little ones who died here last winter. The procession limped disjointedly along, the children doing their best to keep step with no fife or drum, but singing "John Brown's body lies a-mouldering in the grave" and bearing aloft, tied to a fish pole, a diminutive flag, borrowed, for the occasion, from the school Doctor. As the procession passed, we followed, and when the little girls placed the wreaths they had made upon the soldiers' graves, we saw your Scotch friend, whom the Indians call "Mack," suddenly draw a handkerchief from his pocket and turn his back upon us all.

* * *

Chief Joseph came to see the Allotting Agent at Lapwai. He cannot be persuaded to take his land upon the Reservation. He will have none but the Wallowa valley, from which he was driven; he will remain landless and homeless if he cannot have his own again. It was good to see an unsubjugated Indian. One could not help respecting the man who still stood firmly for his rights, after having fought and suffered and been defeated in the struggle for their maintenance.

Unidentified Nez Perce woman and boy (*Idaho Historical Society*)

Annie Monteith, a Nez Perce woman, with horse bearing a squaw saddle and decorated for a parade (*Idaho Historical Society*)

"Camp Bearing Tree." Joe Briggs, James Stuart, and Alice Fletcher (*Idaho Historical Society*)

"Mrs. Lawyer winnowing, Kamiah" (*Schlesinger Library, Radcliffe College*)

"Camp McBeth in smoke." Alice Fletcher on the doorstep of Sue McBeth's cabin near Kamiah *(Idaho Historical Society)*

"Camp on Craig Mountain," Alice Fletcher, Joe Briggs (right), and chainman (*Idaho Historical Society*)

Schoolboys gathered at graves of soldiers in Lapwai on Decoration Day (*Schlesinger Library, Radcliffe College*)

"Chief Joseph," James Stuart and Alice Fletcher with the famous leader (*Idaho Historical Society*)

Joseph speaks very little English but understands more: he is to see us again at Kamiah.

* * *

Having some land business to transact in the vicinity of the Roman Catholic mission, the Allotting Agent planned to go on Corpus Christi day, that we might witness the procession and see the purple vestments of the Bishop who came at that time to gather up his tithes.[19] The Indians contribute to the church of their adoption in their usual generous manner. We have been told that the Bishop took away about six hundred dollars, but we cannot vouch for this statement. It seems a liberal sum when one takes into account the extreme poverty, but the Indians pay well for everything they buy. They never haggle about prices and if they wanted to buy their own souls, or save that of a friend, I have no doubt they would do it in a generous spirit: it is their way.

The holy priests are also generous in their dealings with their Indian converts. They are wiser than some of us. They do not wrench the man too suddenly from all he has hitherto held sacred. They have the art to combine: to make an easy sliding scale upon which the "Heathen Indian" can almost unconsciously slip into a good Catholic.

While a very sensible and learned priest was telling me that "The Indians are children and must be amused and we get up these spectacles to amuse them," I watched the procession which wound along between rows of transplanted cedar trees, with here and there, little shrines where bright colored pictures of saints gave a festive touch to the scene; and I wandered back in memory to the twenty-four hours we once spent without fatigue in the red man's own cathedral, the Mystery Lodge, amid its wealth of color, song and ritual: and I hoped that, in the religion represented before us, there were other compensating features, for in the way of entertainment, it certainly fell far short of the native production. Perhaps the miscarriage of many of our efforts in behalf of the race comes from our ignorance of its own ideals. But now the Indians, clothed in the best they had, marched solemnly behind the priests and the Bishop, singing as they went; a gruesome sound, but suited to the solemn purpose they had in hand, for they were going to "shoot a devil," so the man who carried the gun told us afterward. He exploded it at certain points along the line of march and the noise of it seemed to edify the whole company. I have no doubt it killed a devil, but, as the Cook said, "What is one devil, more or less, on a Reservation?"

* * *

And now came the summer days, all busy days, from sunrise, when the Indian made his descent upon our quarters, until nightfall, when he mounted his pony and loped away up the trail and down upon all our worldly belongings, thick as the cares which beset us, but more easily dislodged. But the thermometer marked a steady rise of temperature, and the time to migrate at length arrived and we must go over the mountains to Kamiah.

Letter Sixteen

Kamiah, N.P.R.
August 15, 1890

[The previous year Alice Fletcher had promised to finance the restoration of the Kamiah Presbyterian Church.]

. . . The morning after our arrival in Kamiah, Old Billy had called to pay his respects and to say that the Indians had done their part; that the "shakes" were split out, the lumber for the repair of the church was hauled from the mill, and the nails were on the ground. Everything was waiting for the fulfillment of our promise to put the dilapidated building in order. . . .

On the first Sunday of our return to Kamiah, we all went to church, with the significance of our promise stirring our conscience as the soundest sermon never had done. Not that we did not mean to fulfil it to the letter; we would, though as the Cook saw we should have to go through the burning fiery furnace to do it, and it looked, that July day, as if the furnace was getting ready for us.

Last year, we had worshipped in an unknown tongue in that little church. It was easy to be devout in the company of those reverent Indians. There was a pervading spirit which transported us out of our surroundings, and our hearts and eyes were filled with the beauty we could not see and our ears vibrated with a melody we did not hear. Now, under the pressure of that tormenting promise, our hearts were as heavy as lead, and when we came out, even the Photographer had nothing better to say than "That building is enough to chill the devotion of anybody but an Indian." The poor little box! some twenty by forty feet in size, with a rough floor and ceiling of boards painted a pink blue, with walls of paper (pasted on cloth, as is the fashion in the far west,) split and torn in all directions and of two distinct patterns and colors, although that was not now noticeable, both having grown so dim with age and smoke and dust. The benches had once been painted blue and there were green shades to the windows. The pulpit, made after the similitude of a dry goods box and mounted upon a platform two steps high, was painted white with sky blue panels. The top of the pulpit was on a level with the collar-bones of the preacher and was surmounted by a section of inclined plane which left the top of his head visible to the congregation.

Behind the pulpit, a drapery of the Ten Commandments, on white cotton muslin, was tacked to the wall at the two upper corners, and on either side of it hung one of those brilliant Sunday school lesson exponents, descriptive of some striking point in Jewish history or mythology done in colors. For instance, a vivid blue Abraham offering up a scarlet Isaac upon a yellow altar and a purple whale swallowing a blue Jonah in an ultramarine sea. Each Sunday Old Billy changed these object lessons, and then David in green breech cloth would be standing upon a prostrate Goliath in yellow, in the act of cutting off his vermillion head; or Daniel, in a red Roman toga, would be on his knees before a goodly company of Vandyke brown wild beasts in a raw-sienna cave. Such barbaric things Christian men and women send to the gentle savage to teach him that there once lived a race more barbarous than his own! And there they still hung that first Sunday of our return. The faithful Billy had turned a leaf, cutting off Joshua and his paralyzed orb of day and bringing up the Witch of Endor; blotting out the pink-limbed Adam and Eve in their pea-green garden and calling Cain and Abel upon the peaceful scene.

We shuddered as we gazed at the pictures, but the Indians sang on undismayed and, while they sang, Her Majesty was thinking hard. Something *must* be done for this people to put a bit of beauty in their worship of a beauty-loving God. . . .

At the close of the service, notice was given that a meeting would be held on the morrow, at our cabin, to plan out the work, and the Indians were invited to come with all the advice and assistance at their disposal; and then we went home to consider the serious practical features of the situation which never strike impulsive people squarely in the face, but are cumulative, growing more and more, as you wrestle with the problem. And this was our problem: given a pile of rough lumber, two kegs of nails, three kegs of paint, a lump of putty, a box of glass, forty rolls of wall paper, a white wash brush, a box of carpenter's tools, a spade, an iron bar, and four pairs of hands already full: this at one end of the equation: at the other, a fallen-to-pieces church to be "made as good as new."

Yes, that was just what we had promised and the whole congregation was confidently waiting to see us do it. I pass over the humiliating spectacle of our dissensions over the matter. I will not say that Briggs insisted that he couldn't undertake any outside job while in the service of the United States; how James declared that he "never had no time for nothing;" how the Photographer diligently shut himself up in his dark room; how Her Majesty said "really her sense of duty would not allow *her* to drive nails into any extraneous matter, even if she could drive nails at all." I will simply state that, with remarkable unanimity, the Cook was decided to be the only independent and available member of our community and that she ought and must shoulder the responsibility.

"Of course," said the Surveyor, "I can pitch in for a couple of hours in the morning." (He always rose before dawn.) "And then the Fourth of July; you are welcome to that, and when it rains."

"It never rains in July," said the Cook.

"We will make the Indians help a good deal," said Her Majesty. "Yes," feebly responded the Cook, and James added, "I guess I can find time to build the belfry." He said it in a melancholy tone, but the Cook knew that James had set his heart upon making that belfry: that he had drawn innumerable plans for its construction, that he had boasted to more than one Indian of his especial ability in the matter of belfries; and yet the Cook cooly answered the Driver and Interpreter that "Luke could make the belfry." (Luke was the brother of Robert and the Cook's particular friend.) But the more she said that Luke could do it, the more James found that he had time at his disposal. He, too, could get up at dawn and work several hours before Her Majesty would need his service, and Her Majesty herself declared that she could also rise before it was day, should it be necessary. "And I suppose," muttered the Cook, "I shall need to stay up all night."

But things shaped themselves after a little turmoil and vexation of the spirit. Briggs tried faithfully to get ahead of the Cook and have his breakfast out of her way before she should come upon the scene with her coffee pot, but he rarely succeeded: her breakfast was initiated beneath the stars and the dawn assisted at its consummation.

It was not easy to stir the Indians up to the point of actual physical exertion. They would come, a few of them, and lie on the grass and watch Briggs as he made notes of what was to be done, but they could not be persuaded to move themselves. When the Surveyor introduced his bulky person under the building to inspect the foundation, they thought it a good joke, and lay on the grass and laughed. When James was bidden to tell them they must help, they laughed some more. When informed that some logs must be brought for a new foundation, they continued to lie on the grass and laugh.

"What do they say?" asked Briggs.

"They do not say anything."

Then Briggs would shoulder his theodolite and march away to his surveying and the Cook would go back to the little cabin to find Her Majesty sitting serenely at her table, writing or registering a group of Indians who sat about the door or lay upon the ground as if time and eternity were at their disposal and life's first duty was to take it easy. Upon such a peaceful scene the Cook would enter, hot and worried, to throw off her sun bonnet and sit down to wonder "Could ever anything overcome the inertia of the people and would any good result from its overcoming, even if it were possible to find a motive strong enough?" At such times nothing seemed worth doing and it was in her heart to find an excuse even for the *laissez-faire* Indian policy.

Things went on in this way for several days until an idea seemed to strike Her Majesty, and she said, "James, what is the matter? What makes the Indians act so; don't they want to help about the church? Don't they want it repaired? What did they bring the lumber for? Have they changed their minds?"

"There's a split," said James solemnly.

"A what?"

"A split, since you went away."

"A split in the church, you mean?"

"Yes, some of them are against Robert." (Robert was the native preacher.)

"What has he done?"

"Don't know; they're all in it."

"All who?"

"All the people: they're afraid."

"What of?"

"The old chiefs won't let the church be repaired, because they say you are doing it for Robert; and they hate Robert."

"Why?"

"Oh, they say he brought the allotment upon them. He

was the first to take his land; and because he tells the people there are no more chiefs but all the people are equal, all citizens, and the chiefs are no better than the rest and have to obey the laws just the same."

"And the people who would like to help are afraid, are they?"

"Yes."

"And these Indians who sit on the grass and laugh belong to the chiefs' party and are against Robert?"

"Yes."

"And they come every day and sit there so as to prevent the work?"

"Yes."

"Very well; we will see about that. The church *will* be repaired if I have to send to Mt. Idaho for white men to do it. Who brought the lumber from the mill?"

"Old Billy Williams."

"And the nails and paint from Lewiston?"

"Old Billy."

"And who split out the shakes for the roof?"

"Luke and Robert."

"Then everything so far has been done by the Williams family?"

"Yes."

"And where is Felix and the rest of *your* uncles?"

"At home."

"Are they afraid?"

"I don't know."

"Well, go and tell Felix I want to see him, and Robert, and every body else you can find. Who belong to the chiefs' party?"

"All the police and the Agency Indians and Archie Lawyer; he is the worst of all."

Now Archie Lawyer is a native minister of the Gospel, ordained before he had experienced a change of heart.[20] He is an intriguing fellow with no character to lose; always in mischief and in debt, always determined to lead somebody someway. If he possessed less wit, he would not be so dangerous; as it is, his influence is pernicious in the extreme. He stands for the power of the old chiefs as Robert stands for simple right and justice and godliness; and Robert was the object of special persecution.

Robert came to see us on the evening of the day in which James had enlightened Her Majesty, and we sat on the rickety steps to our cabin and, bit by bit, we drew from him what had happened in the Vale of Kamiah during the winter of our absence. Her Majesty said, "The people do not seem to want to repair the church now; they will not help."

"Aah."

"Is it because they do not like you?"

"I think."

"What makes you think so?"

"They say guilty to me."

"I do not understand, Robert."

"I tell you. When you came to Kamiah last, you know, I sick; hand cut bad, you know?"

"Yes, I remember, Robert. You came to see me with it in a sling."

"Yes; that time very sick; not work: woman came to my house, my wife gone. Harry Hays at my house; woman cook for us. She stay all night; Harry stay too. The woman go away and sometime she take Cowly. You know Cowly?"

"Yes, he has worked for me."

"Bad woman. Cowly join church and he sorry because of the woman. I speak to woman and she angry. She go away and tell Agent and Judges one lie; she accuse me that night she stay at my house two, three month before she take Cowly. All the people listen to the woman. Nobody ask me. Then old Chiefs call council one night. All chiefs come; they all say, 'Robert guilty.' Then the Chief call council of all the old men one night. They come and the Chiefs say, 'Is Robert guilty?' and they tell the old men if anybody say *not* guilty, they will punish him all the same as Robert. The old men afraid; they all say, 'Robert guilty.' Then they call the young people and say, 'Is Robert guilty?' and the young men all say Robert guilty."

"And did no one stand up for you?"

"Solomon, he say Robert not guilty; all the rest afraid."

"What under Heaven," said the Cook, "are they afraid of?"

Robert smiled. "It is the old thing," he said. "They do not know the Chiefs have no longer power to hurt; the people are in bondage."

"What did they do next?"

"The policeman come to my house and say, 'Robert, come!' I go with policeman. He take me to old school-house,—you know?"

"Yes," said the Photographer, "I have my dark room there."

"They make big fire in stove; they say, 'We punish you' and they hold me over red hot stove long time."

"And you let them do it! Why did you not fight, Robert?"

"Jesus did not fight," said Robert; and there was a little pause in the questioning. "Besides," continued he, "I could not resist. It was a policeman in the uniform of the Government who held me over the stove. I was very sick; I said, 'I faint, my brother, let me go.' They said 'No, we punish you.'"

"Was Felix there?"

"Yes."

"And he did not interfere?"

"No, he afraid. Felix good man. Somebody said, 'Let him go now,' and they put me out in the snow. It storm much that night."

"Where did you go, Robert?"

"I got on my horse and went to Mt. Idaho to Miss McBeth. I was very sick. Miss McBeth thought I die. I had pneumonia."

"And why did you not have the ringleaders arrested?" said the Cook.

"Oh, it is only one little thing. They punish me many times. I die some day; it is all over. I fight Chiefs' power always. I speak to make the people free; sometime all free: I die happy."

"Robert, you did not preach last Sunday?"

"No, I cannot preach; Presbytery say 'no.'" Then he told

us what I have already written you of the proceedings at Lapwai.

"Do you think, Robert," said Her Majesty, "that the Agent knew about your persecution?"

"I don't think," said Robert. "He knew something; not all. Old Chiefs' party shake hands with Agent all the same both."

"And you cannot preach for six months?"

"No. When church all done, I go preach in Lemhi country."

"Well," said the Cook, standing up very straight as was her wont when her mind was made up, "the church will be repaired. We will make a new start tomorrow." Robert smiled.

"Good!" said he. "We make church house for God. I not preach; all right. Somebody preach; all right."

Her Majesty held a council that night and something she said cemented the whole force into one determination. At four o'clock the next morning the Cook was wakened by a queer ripping kind of noise from the direction of the church. It took but a moment to make her toilet and put her oatmeal upon the fire and rush out to reconnoitre. There, upon the roof, she saw Briggs tearing off old shingles with a vigor which hither-to had lain dormant in his makeup. His example had vivified James, who was wielding an old hoe and making the dust fly as if pursued by a tornado. Two or three Indians and a chainman or two were also assisting in a milder way; and actually, before it was time to take the field, the roof of that little church stood denuded to the bare boards. By nine o'clock, little groups of astonished red men gazed up awe struck; some, like the enemies of Nehemiah, counselling resistance, and others, too inert to think of doing anything, lay upon the grass and ridiculed the undertaking. On one side of the church sat Robert Williams diligently shaving the shakes. He had already finished a little heap and his serious smile expressed the faith manifested by his work. There is persuasive power in the example of a steady unassuming persistence in well doing. It was not long before other willing hands were helping Robert; and by and by, Felix appeared and, as an Elder in the church, took a sort of direction of the work. Old Billy rigged up a drag, harnessed his horses to it and brought, one by one, six heavy logs from the mill where they had lain for years, waiting to be cut by the Government miller into boards for the Indians' use in building their little cabins. These were donated by their owner to renew the sills which were rotted away. When this was done, Billy started for the Agency to borrow jack screws; sixty five miles over such as trail as you, my dear N., never travelled, and then Her Majesty appeared upon the scene and ordered Tobias and Sanballet to go to work or to mount their horses and go away. Some did the one thing and some the other, though none were under the slightest obligation to do either. It was hard at first to manage the conflicting elements, but a good working order was gradually evoked. Some, willing to work, did not know how, and had to be taught by the expenditure of much time and strength as the work itself required, but no proffered help could be refused. Then there were not tools enough and Her Majesty had to buy hammers and borrow hatchets and every purchase meant a trip to Mt. Idaho.

Luke was made foreman of the carpenters and Briggs was advisory counsel. He showed the Indians how to cut the logs and, one day when the sun refused to cast a shadow, he set up the jack screws and when the Indians saw the building rise inch by inch, into something like perpendicularity, their interest in the work grew, and the new sills were quickly put in place: and then, half a dozen young men volunteered to nail the shingles upon the roof. The noise of the busy hammers made the Cook's heart glad. She declared that "It was better than an Oratorio."

Meanwhile, Robert sat busy at work in his heap of shavings until, overcome by the great heat, he fainted at his post.

Some of the Sanballet crew tried to terrify the Indians by asserting that Robert was sunstruck by an angry Providential dispensation, but he returned to his work, and row by row, the roof came out in its fresh cedar dress. Then the belfry timbers were bolted on and James astonished the Cook so that she forgot to go home to make the hash for dinner until long past sunset, for he mounted the roof with his tools and could not be coaxed down until it was pitch dark,—too late to drive a nail or saw a joint.

After the work of her day was over, Her Majesty would walk out to view the progress and give new inspiration to the workers. It is hard to resist praise, though one can be defiant against blame. The Indians who would not work slunk away when Her Majesty commended the others and the willing hands multiplied, until even old Wilson, a staunch Roman Catholic, drove several nails into the Presbyterian edifice. Some very old men begged for something to do and the Cook gave old Isaac some putty to soften. He sat down under a tree with a little group around him and softened and moulded the putty into a very good likeness of a pig with its tail curled and a stick in its mouth. Then he came to the Cook, who was setting glass in the window frames, and laid the pig down softly and slipped away. Of course she was very much surprised and very much afraid of that pig, whereat all the children laughed heartily, and wanted more putty to soften.

Billy, when he saw the roof open, and the seats out under the trees, and the sash piled up in a heap, and the rotten porch torn away, had his faith sorely tried. He saw the work of destruction, but could see no farther. One day, he looked cautiously into the church and beheld the Cook, with saw and hammer, attacking the sacred pulpit. It was too much for the old man. He fled, and never again did he venture where his profaned eyes could behold this wholesale desecration.

Of the struggle going on in Billy's breast between the evidence of his senses and his faith in us, he gave no sign. Outwardly, he was still the same placid, loveable old man, smiling benignly when we chanced to meet, but lingering no longer affectionately about the premises; his rapid, noiseless steps passed by at a distance and his face was turned the other way.

But at length our work approached the end. The Cook had remodelled the pulpit and grained it with a high mahogany finish and painted two chairs and a table, of Luke's construction, to match. The "platform" was carpeted in red to harmonize with the plush cushion and the ten Command-ments were nicely framed and hung against the wall. What the walls of that little church house had cost, may you never know by like experience. . . . The last nail had been driven in the weather boarding, the sash was reglazed, the inside wood work mended and cleaned, and the belfry stood out sharply defined against the sky. . . .

Some good women of the tribe, who had volunteered to clean the old pews, thought they could also paint them. They did their best and, luckily, the paint held out.

Several willing old men also eagerly offered to paint the weather boards, and before they finished they had learned that it was not economical to fill the brush with paint and let the surplus drip off upon the ground. The knowledge will be worth something to them in the future for already we hear that several of the little home cabins are to have a beautifying touch when the money is saved up to buy the paint.

But now our petty trials were all over, our promises made good. The bell rope hung in the vestibule, the window shades were in place, the floor washed, the plush cushion with the big Bible on it, the ground cleared of rubbish and then Her Majesty sent for Old Billy.

He came in shyly, walked down to the pulpit, put his hand on the Bible, touched the carpeted platform and the table and the chairs, then winking hard, he walked all round the room touching every seat and came at last to the bell.

"Ring the bell, Billy," said the Cook, and the old man grasped the rope and gave it a strong pull. He did not know how to let it slip between his fingers, and was carried off his feet. But he rang the bell again and again, and then, turning to us, he said, while tears ran from his blinking eyes, "Now I die happy. God got a good church house."

Billy disappeared the next day, but came back with a new broom, which he had ridden to Mt. Idaho, twenty-five miles distant, to buy; and you may be sure that no dust will be allowed to stay in that precious church, and woe to the small boy who scratches beast or bird on one of those new painted pews. . . .

Letter Seventeen

In the Field,
Camp near Cottonwood[21]
September 21st, 1890

. . . Did you ever think how simple the process of living really is, if you divest it of the esthetic element which so complicates it with you? Brought down to the level of corporeal necessity, how very few indeed are the actual wants of a human being; they are but the vital needs of any other animal. . . .

We rise with the sun, perforce, and the first sounds that fall upon our ears are those made by the fire maker outside, then the bubbling of the water in the camp kettle, and the Cook goes out to find the coffee pot waiting upon a hot stone for her manipulations. Her Majesty orders the blankets taken out and spread in the sunshine where they lie all day and are brought in fresh and warm before the cool of the evening.

Before the morning meal is well out of the way, Indians begin to come and Her Majesty's work commences before you have finished your "beauty sleep." It is a long day before the last Nez Perce mounts his pony and gallops away and in that day one or two little trips of a few miles may have been taken, half a dozen knotty cases settled and the intricacies of relationship traced through several obscure families, with much plotting and writing of letters in the chinks of time.

Now imagine us at sunset,—the work of the day over, the schedules and maps and books put out of sight, the blankets well shaken lest some rattlesnake hide therein and preempt our bed; the camp fire replenished and we gathered about our frugal board. It is literally a board and there are tin cups and tin plates upon it to say grace over. We sit on an upturned horse bucket, a bag of oats, the camera box, or a pile of stones: we are not over fastidious in this respect. . . .

* * *

Our camp at this time is pitched within ten miles of a Post Office. If you could but know it, you are only ten days distant from this camp of ours. Her Majesty has gone to allot a group of progressive Indians some 20 miles away. It will be late before she returns and Miss Kate will be with her. We shall dine by the light of the moon and gossip around the camp fire. In honor of the occasion I shall have the tent floor strewn with clean straw and the tin ware introduced to Sapolio. I cannot think of any other possible concession to the proprieties of polite life.

We have had a good many uninvited guests of late. Three nights ago a drove of wild horses raided our camp and a wolf came down to steal a ham which the Cook had hung up in a tree too high for his wolfship. Whether he entered the tent or no I cannot say, but, from the appearance of the flour bag, I think he did. . . .

* * *

We have bid a final adieu to Kamiah. We left no aching hearts behind us as has sometimes happened when the pale face has finally turned away from the Indian's home, and we know that no one will be the worse for our coming. We have swept out all traces of our occupancy from the little missionary's cabin; the goldenrod has gone to seed and the pole cat is dead. It was the only living thing that came out to greet us upon our first arrival in the valley and it grew to have a strong attachment for us. It made its home under the cabin, coming out at twilight and waddling about Her Majesty's feet as she mused in the gathering darkness on the doorstep. The Photographer has often tried in vain to snap a shot at its broad back as it glided quickly from its hiding place in the wake of a wandering chicken, or ran swiftly along the path to the river; and now it was gone forever. . . .

Letter Eighteen

CAMP PRAIRIE CHICKEN
September 24th, 1890

We have a new worry sprung upon us. Briggs has had a position on the N.P.R. [Northern Pacific Railroad] offered him which is so much better than the one he holds with us, that we are in a selfish panic. The idea of his leaving at this time is appalling, for who could take up his work? An expert would find it not an easy task, but think of the material really available in this locality! The surveyor whose works have mostly followed him on this Reservation is the man who has been entirely superior to field observations; who has made notes in his office and plotted the ground under the inspiration of his own imagination.

Tracts of worthless, rocky wastes and barren hilltops have been described as arable land and allotted to Indians in 20 acre lots, when it is evident that the surveyor could never have been on the spot. One of the greatest impediments to the right prosecution of the Nez Perce work at this time lies in the inaccuracies of the survey Her Majesty is expected to follow. And the shifts she has had to make in towing her surveyor in other fields would, if detailed, make an interesting book to read.

I recall one man that the impossibility of replacing caused us to treat with careful consideration. He was employed to retrace a former survey.

"Where is the section corner, Mr. Jonas?" Her Majesty would say.

"Wall, it orter be somewhere round here, dont you think?" And he would begin a series of gyrations about an imaginary centre, and revolve, and revolve, concentrically, until he narrowed down his orbit to a rotary motion about his own bootheel. Sometimes he found the corner stone, but oftener he missed it, and then Her Majesty would suggest the compass.

Jonas was willing to try the compass to please Her Majesty but he said it would not work when the wind blew, and the wind nearly always blew on that Reservation. He relied more upon his unaided "squint"; he "could squint just as well without the instrument as with it": so, putting his hands upon either side of his nose, to cut off the side light, he would move on, and Her Majesty would follow in the buggy, measuring the distance by counting the revolutions of the hind wheels, one of which was marked by a handkerchief tied about a spoke.

That kind of surveying would not do on the N.P.R. (Nez Perce reservation) with its cañons and mountains, and so we are anxious about Briggs. We appreciate his good qualities as never before; we find new depths to his angelic patience, and one can see that the Cook, though she scorns to be sentimental, pays particular attention to the brewing of the soup, when the Surveyor is near enough to sample her achievement.

I wonder if you have ever felt the stillness of a night out alone with Nature? Not that it is ever absolutely still, but there is no fog of sound for a background, as in a town. What noises there are, are distinct and break upon your ear as the stars upon your eye in a cloudless night. We were lying awake the night after Briggs had told us of his business offer, wakeful with anxiety, when the quick, sharp dick of a pony's foot startled us. We knew that an Indian had forded the Clearwater and was coming nearer and nearer: we could distinguish, from the sound, the very nature of the ground passed over.

Now he is coming up from the ford, the feet patter on the stones, now they thud on the turf, and then—a cry rings out on the empty air. "Wako Felixnim ewapna saiau he, etu imim sap-a-lik-nikt a-ke-you!" It is echoed and reechoed among the hills and cañons and dies away long after the horseman has passed our cabin on his way to carry the news to all the people.

"Now Felix' wife is asleep, do what you have to do!"

In the morning, we asked James what it meant: "do what you have to do," and he told us that Felix wanted his wife to be buried as white people are and that he, James, had promised to make a coffin.

But "Etu imim sap-a-lik-nikt a ke you" kept on ringing in our ears until Her Majesty ordered out the horses and drove up to the desolated home. When she returned she brought with her some white muslin which Felix had bought with an indistinct idea of its use in the "white woman's burial" he so much desired for his beloved wife.

"We must be gratified in his pathetic little wish," said Her Majesty, and so we ransacked our wardrobes to supplement Felix' material, and when the robe was finished, we went up the valley to help at the last simple rites.

The body, upon a new white blanket, lay on the ground beneath an awning. About it the women were grouped, while a little apart, two or three young men were preparing a coffin. When it was finished, Her Majesty lined it with the muslin and the Cook went out on the hillside to gather something in the way of flowers to relieve its bare pine boards. She came back with a handful of golden rod and some fir branches: there was nothing else to be found growing in the parched soil.

The women sat silently watching while we arranged this "white woman's burial," so pitiful in its poverty of resources, wondering all the while what those calm, solemn faced people were thinking there in the presence of their dead. What, to them, was the significance of the coffin? Was not the new white blanket of their own custom better? Did the white people not know that the shut up box would hinder the spirit from going to its own place? And why the pleated muslin and the white gown and the golden rod and the silence? Would not their own old funeral song cheer the departing spirit more truly? Were the white people's ways better for the Indian than his own?

The unmoved faces of the women told us nothing: Were they dumb all through? Who could tell?

Felix sat in his house with a few of the old men, waiting.

At last when all was ready, the people gathered together under the trees and the native pastor lifted up his hands and a prayer was spoken in Nez Perce; and now there was wonderful light in the dumb faces and, as the prayer moved on,— we could not understand,—but it seemed as if those Christian Nez Perces must break out in triumphant song. But the song followed in repressive English and, after a short reading from the Bible and a few words of sympathy and consolation and hope from the pastor, the body was carried in reverent silence to the grave.

Two days after the funeral, Felix appeared at our camp to bid us goodbye. He was going to the mountains. It was so lonely in his home; he would not be back until the snow fell. Until the snow fell! We did not grasp the idea very quickly, for we were struggling for breath in a stiffling smoke laden atmosphere.

The mercury was 101° the next day when we started out to find Briggs' camp to settle some disputes about allotments.

We were so unwise as to go without our tent, hoping to occupy a little new cabin which the owner had placed at our disposal but the surveying party had preempted it. They were all in the field when we arrived and entered so unexpectedly upon their housekeeping. If Briggs had realized that the Photographer was liable to bring his camera upon the scene, he would not have left so picturesque a view open to him, and if the chainmen had anticipated a visit from Her Majesty, they would have left a square inch unoccupied somewhere.

But a branch of fir tree soon swept out a corner, saddles and blankets and frying pans were forced into closer proximity, and then our conquered territory, curtained off with our wagon tarpaulin, make us a very comfortable camping place, and we were in no wise disturbed when, later on, our family was increased by seven Indians, four white men and a dog.

The mercury fell to 45° in the night and we rose early to warm ourselves by exercise. Then a table was improvised and the Surveyor and the Special Agent plotted and allotted for several hours, while the Indians gathered, until the Cook began to think that her provision for only one day's need was a grave mistake. But we had time to tumble back down into Kamiah before dark. These little trips are exhausting for familiarity with Standing Gulch has not bred in us a contempt for its threatening dangers or insensibility to its actual pains.

Briggs says we call it Standing Gulch because it stands on end, but Briggs is wrong for once. Not that we dispute his premises; the gulch does stand on end with a slight inclination to the horizon at the top, but we call it by the name of the man who came out of that gulch one fine day a month ago and appeared at our cabin door, with a good sized allotment of Nez Perce land upon his broad shoulders and an unconquered sparkle in his eye.

How our drooping souls rejoiced at the sight of him! Nothing so good had ever come to us out of that great split in the earth. Since the day we first escaped out of its jaws, it had been prolific of aches and bruises and torn garments, but here was a live man just from the East where the sun rises to bless and not to shrivel as by fire, and he brought with him a bracing whiff of the atmosphere of civilization. When he took off his dust laden hat, there was an aureole about his head and when he stamped the soil from his boots they shone with unearthly lustre in our eyes,—we who had forgotten Day and Martin, out of whose life the "Raven Gloss" had so long ago departed with numerous other glosses once essential to our comfort, but now as if they had never been. Mr. Standing had come from Carlisle to Kamiah in search of school children and was accompanied by Mr. McConville of the Lapwai school.

They told us that when they reached the top of the gulch they stopped and said, "It is impossible to go down here with a wagon": Then they saw the tracks of our wheels and were ashamed to flinch at a road we had traveled. We did not inform them that we had made the descent the day before with a broken tire, tied on with strings and a bit of wire. It was not politic to show an utter disregard of human life even though that life was our own, so we only remarked that "one could make better time coming down than in going up that gulch."

* * *

Time has not lagged with us this season and September crept imperceptibly, and all too soon, upon our camp, and the call from the mountain came before we were ready to go. We wanted a few days of rest in the peace of Paradise, but there could be no rest until our work was done, so we packed our equipage and supplies in a springless farm wagon, harnessed Selim and Jimmy as leaders, the venerable Dick and George as wheelers and tied our ordinary light "buggy" to the freight department.

Then we climbed on top of our cargo behind the driver and set our train in motion. It was 48 feet long ánd the Photographer said he could not get a view of it except as a panorama. We did not attempt the Standing Gulch though we had, in avoiding it, to wind in and out of box cañons, go up and over mountains, ford deep streams and wade through shifting sand.

But, with an Indian on horse-back to watch that all went well and give the alarm when the tied behind "buggy" slewed down the steep hillside or was caught by a projecting tree, and with another Indian to ride in advance to find a way (for there was no road) and to take down a section of fence when we had to cross a field, we arrived without disaster by nightfall at Camp Corbett on the Clearwater River, about half way out of the cañon.

The two great events of this camp were a hen for supper and a visit from James' grandmother, a very old woman whose memory was stored full of folklore and bits of thrilling history of her tribe. To look at the little woman whose face was fearfully marred and scarred by hard fortune, whose hands and feet were petite and delicately shaped, who was graceful in motion and courteous in manner, one would be slow to give credence to her tales of the war exploits in which she had borne an active part. Human nature is very complex. Here was this gentle hearted old Indian, who would not taste food until she had asked her God's blessing upon it, tender as a child in her affectionate confidence, and yet bearing the well-earned reputation of "fierce and strong."

Briggs joined us at Camp Corbett. Another day's journey would bring us to his camp on the uplands and he and his party of chainmen, mounted on their ponies, would follow in the wake of our caravan. But at the first steep incline our tied behind "buggy" slewed down the side of the trail, caught on a stump and stopped all further progress. The leaders plunged, Dick balked and the whole 48 feet of "outfit" seemed about to retrograde to Camp Corbett. Now a backward movement is never on the mind of either the Cook or Her Majesty or even on the Photographer's if it implies special exertion, so after the attachment between the two wagons had given way three times, we decided to walk up the trail, leaving James and one of the chainmen to bring up the disabled caravan.

It was late in the afternoon, but there would be a young moon and, trusting to meet Briggs, who took a rougher cut across the hills, we set off in good spirits. But when all sight and sound of our horses had died out of the landscape and the coyotes began to howl over the hills and the shadows of the spectral pine trees grew so dreadfully long, Her Majesty began to feel tired and less confident. Passing a cabin, she tried to induce an Indian to go with us as guide, but he shook his head and cheerfully said, "Too late; you'll die!" He spoke but little English and all we could make out of him was— that at the top of the first hill there were two trails, one of which was the one to be taken while the other was not "tots" (good).

"Instructions as clear as a Government treaty with the Indians," said the Cook, "but we will not go back now."

"Suppose we wait for James to overtake us," said Her Majesty.

"There will be nothing left of us but bones by that time," said the Cook as the multitudinous howl of a coyote close by startled the loneliness into frightful echoes, "come on, James may not come this way at all."

The first half mile was steep and exhausting and at the end of it were the two diverging trails. While halting to decide which not to take, the portly figure of Briggs loomed up against the sky and a quick "halloo" attracted his attention. Blessed old Briggs! His jocund face was like that of an angel in its opportuneness. "I was looking for you," he said, as he led his horse up beside the Cook. "My land! it's too bad!" and he insisted that Her Majesty and the Cook should ride his faithful horse.

They would not both together weigh so much as his usual load and "the animal was quite fresh," he said. He lifted the Cook into the saddle, but Her Majesty hung back. There were some positions, she insisted, where even the moral support of the Cook could not give her a feeling of security. She could not be persuaded. She sat down upon a stump and Briggs thrust his theodolitic tripod into the ground and mused.

"Tom'll do it," at length he said,—Tom was the horse— and grasping the long tail of the animal, he braided it into a smooth rope which he placed in Her Majesty's hands, bidding her to "Hold on tight," then, shoulder[ing] his theodolite, and putting an arm through the reins, he led the way through the gathering darkness, over the blind trail. . . .

But the moment arrived when the Special Agent could no longer "hold on." One after another the glossy black strands slipped through her nerveless fingers and Tom stopped and turned his wise old head to see what had become of his precious charge. Then the Cook vowed and protested, as she slipped off the saddle into a furrow of newly plowed field we were crossing, that the Allotting Agent must and should ride the rest of the way, or we would all be responsible for her death and the long train of calamities which would ensue.

It was not difficult to lift the now unresisting Special Agent into the saddle,—she always gave up gracefully having her own way when it had been demonstrated that she could not help herself,—and Briggs searched his pockets for an inspiration to an additional stirrup. He pulled out a piece of red tape . . . and he tied it as a streamer to Tom's glossy mane.

Meanwhile, Briggs had taken off his silk kerchief and, knotting it to another from the pocket of his blouse, he supported Her Majesty's lame foot, and, walking beside, he held her firmly in the saddle, while the Cook led Tom at such a pace as soon brought us in sight of the camp fire.

This is the one compensating hour in the rough routine of Government work in the field. When the sun has descended below the horizon line and drawn his last lingering ray after him, then the Allotting Agent may safely say to herself in the midst of the espionage of her legions of political enemies, "This hour is mine." None shall dare rise to object to her appropriation of the peace that comes with the sense of duty done at the close of a hard day's work. Nature is not parsimonious, and the meek shall inherit the earth.

There was the sound of bustle and the sight of moving figures in the radius of illumination about Briggs' camp as we drew near. We heard the breaking of dry branches and saw the sparks fly upward against the background of sky and tree, as the fire was replenished in honor of our approach. It was a homecoming, [in] spite of the prospect of waiting for supper and lodging until James should come up with our camp belongings. At Briggs' most sanguine estimate, he could not arrive before midnight, but when has the shifty Surveyor ever balked in his creation of comfort out of the most unpromising material?

He soon contrived a seat for Her Majesty and the Cook on the windward side of the column of smoke and while the warmth gradually started the circulation in their benumbed faculties, he made a loaf of bread in the frying pan and brewed a can of coffee, joking them all the while into good humor and grateful recognition of their mercies.

And there we lingered in dreamy half-consciousness while the chainmen told stories and sang themselves to rest and the stars slipped, one by one, over the edge of the horizon until, at last, James brought in the belated caravan. Many willing hands set up our house for us and tired nature's sweet restorer did not fail in her ministrations. Ears and eyes were soon sealed to the farther intrusion of care, but, alas! for only as long as the sun remained hidden. At the first sign of his awakening, upon our little tent, there was no more sleep for us; no possible pulling down of blinds to piece out the too short night.

There is no way of counterfeiting anything in camp or of evading its bald truth. A new day is upon us and we must rise to its responsibilities.

* * *

Letter Nineteen

LAPWAI
October 28th, 1890

You complain that my letters "are all on a dead level, monotonous and melancholy in tone"; that I am "running the Agency system into the ground, and it is hard reading."

I was so disturbed by your remarks that I went to the Cook for comfort. She said that if my letters were all on a dead level you could hardly expect them to be lively, and as to running the Agency system into the ground, if I only ran it down deep enough, I would be the world's greatest benefactor of the age. When we came to the "hard reading" clause of your indictment, she made light of that, saying that your judgment could not be properly weighed unless it was known how soft the literature was you were accustomed to reading. Everything was comparative, she said. She would advise me to send you a few quotations from our camp literature as a tonic to your vitiated mental appetite.

This is a specimen of what I have read to Her Majesty from half past eight o'clock this morning until five this evening, with a half hour intermission for luncheon. It is now six o'clock and we have finished for the day.

Specimen

Kolkartzot. South half of south east quarter of North half and South East quarter of Lot 15, and the North East quarter and North half of South East quarter of North half of Lot 18; and the North west quarter and north half of south west quarter of north east quarter; And North half and North half of south half of North west quarter of Lot 17; and South west quarter of south east quarter and South half of south west quarter of Lot 16; And the South half of North half of South half of Lot 32; and South half of South half of Lot 31; Section 12, Township 33, Range 3, East. And the North half of the North half and North half of South half of North half of Lot 1; And North half of South half of North half of Lot 2, Section 13, Township 33, Range 3, East, And the South half of south half and South half of North half of South half of Lot 9, Section 7, Township 33, Range 4, East, and Lot 4, Section 18, Township 33, Range 4, East.

There! that's good strong literature, but one must read between the lines to feel the real force of it.

It means that Kolkartzot, by virtue of this described allotment, has been raised from the tribal dead level up to United States citizenship with the rights and immunities thereof, subject to the common law of the state in which he lives and protected by its courts. It is hardly to be expected that Kolkartzot will know how to avail him self of his new-born rights. The hope is in the children, and in the loosing of the Agency grip which has succeeded in gelatinizing the Indian's backbone until he lies limp and inert in his degradation.

Lest you should wonder at the complicated description of Kolkartzot's allotment, I must tell you that the law requires land, not rocks, to be given to the Indians. Now to get enough land for Kolkartzot the Surveyor must cut out the ledges which cropped up all over the place where he had his little improvements; bit of good land were scattered in among the rocks and this, and no other, Kolkartzot would have, and as the Indian has the right to choose where he will take his allotment, this is the way it had to be given to him.

Very many allotments among the Nez Perces are of the same character, making the work exceedingly difficult. Sometimes an Indian has parts of his allotment miles distant from each other, thus multiplying the labor of the Surveyor and Special Agent.

* * *

Last week we camped with the Surveying party on the uplands. As we were picking our way down the little gulch where the tents were pitched, Briggs told us how, the first night of their occupancy, they had been obliged to sit up until morning, to guard the small mud hole from the wild stock, in order to keep water enough for their own horses. There was no other within a radius of five miles, and barely sufficient would settle into the hole during the night to supply the necessities of the camp during the day.

The morning after our arrival at Camp Prairie Chicken, (so called from the great numbers of that species which congregated in the neighborhood), the Cook and Her Majesty were alone, for after the surveying party had left, James had to take the horses to Mt. Idaho to be shod and nobody had apparently remembered the precious mud hole.

It was a very hot day and after her legitimate duties were performed, the Cook obligingly offered to assist the Allotting Agent in her clerical work. The two were quietly sitting in the precarious shadow of a tall pine tree, supplemented by the family umbrella, the Cook holding the ink bottle and reading from the field book the allotments which Her Majesty transferred to her plots, when Oresto! upon the crest of the hill opposite, came out sharply against the sky a large "bunch" of wild horses.

Their ears stood up like animated interrogation points and their tails whisked with eager delight as they sniffed the precious mud hole below. The Cook counted forty-five heads and mentally divided one barrel of water into forty-five parts, while Her Majesty jumped up, frantically waving the umbrella and shouting "Shoo! Shoo!" The animated interrogation points grew a trifle more erect and rigid, but there was no sign of a retreat; on the contrary, the squadron moved forward with determination, led by a big buckskin horse, whose tail trailed on the ground and whose nose was high in the air.

There were old horses and young horses, grey mares, and sorrel colts, and more and more appeared upon the ridge in momentary reinforcements.

"What *are* we to do?" inquired the Special Agent.

"Nothing!" replied the irate Cook, who was tired of trying to make up for masculine deficiencies. "The men should have protected the water. What *we* do?"

But Her Majesty was already en route to the field of action and the Cook knew there was going to be a damp Thermopylae, so, armed with James' new horse whip, she followed her leader.

At their decided appearance, the animals paused upon the hill and whisked their tails interrogatively. "Shoo! Shoo!" said Her Majesty. An insolent switch of the big buckskin's tail and a slight onward movement. "Who are you?" said his ears. "I'll let you know," said the Cook with a vigorous snap of her whip, and the squadron halted for farther reconnaissance. It was evident that familiarity would soon breed contempt. The parley could not be prolonged: besides, the most timid creatures become courageous when tormented by thirst. The mudhole lay in a field which had once been fenced in and rails in all stages of decomposition were scattered over an area of a couple of acres.

"If we could only cover up the water with these old rails!" said Her Majesty,—but the water lay in the middle of a well tramped bog,—"How do the men get near enough to dip out the water?"

"Oh, they ride in on their ponies," said the Cook, "or wade in, barelegged."

"If we could build a fence on one side, we could more easily protect the other. You stand here and keep snapping the whip and I'll try," said the Allotting Agent. But it was not in the nature of the Cook to accept this distribution of roles.—"But I cannot snap a whip!" said Her Majesty. "You can wave the umbrella, which will be equally effective," said the Cook. And now, as the exigencies of the situation did not admit much parleying, they both, with one accord, like the Jews under Nehemiah, each with one of her hands wrought in the work and with the other hand held a weapon.

Horses have a good deal of curiosity. Arrested by the strange scene below them, the troop stood spell bound, following with their eyes and ears every movement made by their two determined opponents as they tugged and pulled at the rough rails. They stood until six sections of fence were erected between them and the coveted mud hole. True, it was more like chevaux-de-frise than a well constructed rail fence and it is possible that Buckskin, by one well-directed kick, could have toppled over the whole line. Indeed, as Her Majesty was adjusting the final top rail of the last course, whether her umbrella caught upon the rough end, or whether from unassisted innate depravity often exhibited by inanimate objects, the rail slid off upon the ground, taking Her Majesty's foot in its way, and the jar of its fall caused the whole structure to collapse. In a moment there was nothing to show for all their painful toil but a confused mass of rails, the Special Agent's garments stripped into tatters and the Cook's lacerated hands and mud stained skirts. At this juncture, the squadron on the hill moved leisurely down in solid phalanx.

"We shall be trampled to death in that hasty mire," said the Cook, and she seized both the whip and the umbrella and dashed frantically towards the advancing host. The big buckskin tossed his head, let fly his hind legs, and with a derisive snort, veered off to one side, and, followed by the whole troop, galloped down the ravine, wheeled suddenly about and stood confronting the Cook from the other side of the mud hole.

"We shall have to fence all round the water," said Her Majesty.

"We made the fence too straight," said the Cook; "We were too economical with the rails," and they began to lay them at sharper angles. There was no lack of material, but it lay scattered widely over the field and one must stay to watch the enemy while the other dragged the rails to the scene of action. Horses are very patient animals. These particular horses knew it was only a matter of time when they should again have undisputed possession of their water supply. They even began to nibble the dead grass in the ravine and to bite each other playfully, still, however, keeping their eyes and ears in the direction of the field operations. At length the enclosure lacked only one panel to completion, when an ominous tramp, tramp, announced the approach of a thirsty herd of horned cattle up the ravine.

"Oh, for a dog!" groaned the Cook. She had not thought of wishing for a man, but at this moment one appeared; an Indian on a dappled pony. He stopped, took in the situation at a glance, tied the pony to a rail and in a few moments had completed and strengthened the fence, with a few well directed stones had dispersed the horses and driven back the cattle, and was away, galloping his pony over the hill.

Her Majesty and the Cook retired in a serious mood, to repair damages and talk about the emancipation of women.

"It is largely a matter of clothes," said the former. "And of brute force," said the latter. "Equality of muscular strength is the basic principle," and she spent the rest of the day in extracting the splinters from her hands. She piled nineteen of the largest ones in a sort of memorial cairn on the top of Briggs' theodolite box, wishing they might pierce his conscience when he came to realize the results of his remissness, but Jo, his dog, running into camp in advance, wagged the cairn off with his tail; while the surveying party, with masculine unconcern, pulled down the painfully erected fence and let their horses absorb the last drop of the priceless fluid and then rode away, leaving the rails tramped into the black bog.

The Cook gazed, speechless, until she saw the big buckskin at the head of his squadron coming up the ravine at a leisurely pace, and then she went into retirement to wrestle with her emotions alone. . . .

* * *

We left Camp Prairie Chicken on the morning of September 25th. Our route for the most part was over dry and barren land, where the thirsty cattle roamed, grubbing the roots of the yellow stubble and licking great holes in the salty earth. We had not gone many miles before our caravan broke down. Our forty-eight feet long turnout was too much for the traces and they gave way just as we came in sight of a way side store where we borrowed a chain cable and pushed on. . . .

The next day brought us to Lapwai where Miss Kate had arranged comfortable quarters for us and the School Superintendent, whom the Indians love, has given us a kind welcome to his domain.

Miss Kate has removed from the Agency to this place and is domiciled in the converted root house. We have spent the last few weeks here in office work, interrupted only by a few short trips in the neighborhood for a night's camping. The work of registering the Lapwai Indians drags its slow length along. They have not yet become reconciled to the allotment. The ground gained in Kamiah does not seem to help much here: it looks as if, in a sense, we had to begin all over again.

It requires all Her Majesty's tact to avoid open conflict, for she is constantly meeting decided opposition and in quarters where it would naturally be least looked for; from those Indians nearest the Agency, those most under the influence of the officials. It is not easy to understand some of the obstacles thrown in her way.

One can have unlimited patience with the unreasoning old men whose splendid obstinacy is invincible; who refuse to take their quota of land on principle, holding to their tribal right to roam at will all over the Reservation. It is of no use to explain to *them* that the world is so rapidly filling with people that no tribe can longer hold unused land against the clamor of a multitude of homeless men and women: that the earth, in a sense, belongs to all that are upon it and that no man can be allowed to claim more than he can use for his own benefit or for that of others; that no treaty could be enforced that sought to hold back the living tide that had set in upon this continent: that any tribe of Indians that stood out against that flood would be overwhelmed.

It would be a waste of words to say all this to these superb old colossals, who stand upon their treaty as their own hills upon their basaltic foundations. Nor is it worth while to try persuasion upon the chiefs who, Her Majesty says, "oppose because land in severalty breaks up completely their tribal power and substitutes civilization and law."

But one would expect that the younger men, who have for years been under the enlightening influence of the governing centre of the Reservation, would be able to see that treaties are abrogated by the logic of events. It is also queer that the pupils of that banished missionary up in Mt. Idaho who so disastrously meddled with that mischievous document the Declaration of Independence, should be the most reasonable Nez Perces we have yet encountered and the most loyal to the Government.

Briggs has already bidden us goodbye and gone to Lewiston. As a parting gift he told us that he had decided to finish the allotment survey. He would have his wife and child with him in camp next summer and "business would just hum." . . .

* * *

Our tickets are bought for home via Genesee and the N.P.R. [Northern Pacific Railroad], and tomorrow will see us on the way.

* * *

Letter Twenty

Lapwai
April 30, 1891

. . . We had entered upon the Nez Perce work in ignorance of what had to be done. Not that the simple task of allotting Indian lands was unknown; that was easy enough, but the right of way to it had first to be conquered. Briggs used to say in those first days, "You may lead a horse to the brook

122

"Monday morning in Camp McBeth." Alice Fletcher, Jane Gay, and James Stuart (*Idaho Historical Society*)

"James Reuben and Archie Lawyer" *(Schlesinger Library, Radcliffe College)*

"Joe Kentuck, typical Nez Perce" *(Idaho Historical Society)*

"Retracing a former survey." Alice Fletcher standing with William Caldwell and Abraham Brooks (with cane)—"Blind Abraham." Joe Briggs holds the surveying rod. (*Idaho Historical Society*)

"Camp Sunday." Joe Briggs and Alice Fletcher (*Idaho Historical Society*)

"Some allottees" (*Idaho Historical Society*)

"James' grandmother," Nancy Corbett *(Idaho Historical Society)*

"South Fork of Clearwater River" (Idaho Historical Society)

but you cannot make him drink if he is not thirsty." The Indian was not thirsty. Her Majesty had not only to lead him up to the idea of taking land in severalty, but to make him as an individual *want* to take his own particular allotment. And then, after she had succeeded in exciting so much of interest, came the hardest task of all,—to induce him to *move* in the matter; to go out and personally select his individual inheritance.

He may want to do it, he may will to do it, but the element of time has not entered into his nebulous calculations, with any directive influence. Every thing is large about the Indian; he owns the earth and roams over it and the rising and setting of the sun alone marks his deliberations; he has no clocks or watches to divide time into hours and minutes and it is always undignified to make haste.

To a United States official under bonds for the honest performance of a special duty in its nature reciprocal, depending upon a prompt cooperation, this blurring of the divisions of time is a source of anxiety. We look back over the vista of our achievement as we jog across the continent, returning to the field, and we count it up.

Prejudices broken down, open and covert jealousy of local officials counteracted, the confidence of the tribe practically won, reliable knowledge acquired and everything in train. We have but to go in and occupy; *now* the work will go fast.—Fast! You shall see.

We have been in our old quarters at Lapwai about two weeks, having again come up the Snake river on our old friend the *Annie Nixon.* We needed the restful day of that lovely trip after the weary jolting by rail and before taking up again our work-a-day life.

As we touched the wharf, Briggs, the Surveyor, came on board; and at sight of him the past few months of civilization were as if they had never been. We were again on the Reservation, just where we left off. Briggs told the Cook that there was a new stove in our old quarters at Lapwai. He meant it kindly; it was the best news he had to tell. The Cook took it kindly, but reserved exultation until she had proved the unreliability of her prophetic soul. This was her third year on the Reservation. She was no longer blessed in ignorance of what was before her and knowledge was not power to her. She smiled at the Surveyor as hopefully as she was able and he went on with his news.

It was not all of a pleasant nature. He gave it bit by bit as we rode out from Lewiston to the Fort. "The season was late. Little snow on the mountains promised a dry summer." "The railroad had taken the right of way down the Clearwater river and cut the Indian gardens all to bits, and Cowley was dead." (Cowley was a faithful chainman.) Poor Cowley! "He tried to live until Her Majesty came back."

"Then the Indians were all quarrelling over their land: they could not find the corners."

"Old Jonah and Mrs. P–ka–la–Pikt were on their ear again over a ditch and Captain John was on the war path about his fence." And so we rode on, gathering the alkali dust in our garments and letting down gradually our ideals of beauty and everything else to meet the exigencies of our environment. . . .

Our headquarters are now to be at Lapwai where the Superintendent of the school has made us quite comfortable in an unused building and where Miss Kate looks after our temporal, as well as spiritual welfare. From this point we shall make camping expeditions over a large extent of country. The best lands of the Reservation lie between us and Lewiston and Genesee, and on these the most enterprising Nez Perces we hope may be induced to settle.

We expect a long steady piece of routine work, with little diversion now that novelty is no longer a factor in our lives. But there is an incipient brass band here and the school boys play base ball. We shall get on. . . .

* * *

Letter Twenty-One

LAPWAI
May 30, 1891

We are back at our post of duty and there is nothing new under our sun, except the pine wood fuel, which was cut from the forest last month and sizzles like politics in the "Early Bird" stove and burns when its "ain deil bids it."

But everything else is old: the same old human depravity, old as the creation; old quarrels revamped; old falsehoods, with amendments, to increase their efficiency; and the "Box Case" is the same old fraud with not even a new face upon it. It forced itself upon Her Majesty the day after our first advent upon the Reservation, and it has come round ever since as regularly as the Government Inspector. It is a merry-go-round, at which, after much perturbation, the Indians have learned to laugh. It is a scheme to defraud them of a large tract of their most valuable land, upon which are settled some thirty enterprising Indians.

We are told that the man Box made his appearance in this locality about twenty years ago, bringing with him "from down below" two Indian wives. At the time of his advent, Idaho was taking a start in growth, and the standard of morality in its nascent towns was looking up a little. The enterprising men who were "growing up with the country," along the border of the Reservation, found it desirable to put away their Indian wives and relegate their half breed children to the care of Uncle Sam; and Box negotiated for the transfer, to another man, of one of his two, who was a Dalles Indian woman.

When the Allotting Agent came out to divide the Nez Perce inheritance, Box put in a claim for his retained wife and her large family of children. The discarded wife made no claim at that time, either for herself or her children. She simply said, "I am not a Nez Perce; I have no right to land." Mrs. Box, as she was called, was as wax in the hands of her husband. He said she was a Nez Perce and she tried to be, to the best of her ability.

She could not tell the name of her father and she had no kindred in the tribe, the members of which said her speech was not even equal in diction to the average white man's Nez Perce; but as time went on she found a father who had died before any one could remember him, and claimed relationship with a family, the members of which indignantly repudiated her.

Her Majesty tried to settle the affair which promised to be a source of much trouble, by attempting to induce the Indians to adopt the woman, who being an Indian was entitled to land somewhere, but the people refused upon the ground that the children were such bad characters, some of them being, at the time, under indictment for murder.

The case was sent on to Washington and was decided against Box and the Agent was ordered to put him off the Reservation. The case has been decided several times and reopened as many. Box has been "ordered" off again and again but is still here, putting in a crop and keeping up a friendly intercourse with the Agent.

Queer, is it? No, not at all, from our point of view. Will Box eventually win?

The exasperated Cook says he will.

Her Majesty says "No! There is not a particle of proof of the justice of his claim." But that does not count in the long run and it is the long run that Box is going to make. Officials die every four years, Kings are always arising . . . whose idea of dealing justly is often met in the simple reversal of the acts of their predecessors; who have no time to investigate and whose inclination is always to favor partisan adjustment.

Box is holding on. His last hope is in a change of administration. He has confided his case to a lawyer of what he supposes will be the incoming shade of politics and we are not sure but the Cook has tenable ground for her opinion.

Meanwhile, Her Majesty is harrassed by the Box Case. It

has become a persecution; it haunts her by day and is a burden in her dreams. It comes up again after each defeat in new guise. Just now it has gone to pieces over her Registry, but it is not killed; it will trace a new line of descent and there will be more "trials" and more Inspectors will be sent from Washington to "investigate," and so it goes,—with always a chance that justice may be overridden and fraud prevail.

* * *

The Photographer has become quite chummy with Miss Kate. She seems to have discovered the focal length of his nature and called out the best that is in him. He has been busy lately taking pictures of her Nez Perce woman's industrial society, and he tells us, with more enthusiasm than we supposed he could be capable of, that these few women, with the work of their own unaided hands, have earned money enough to refit the Lapwai Church with new seats tastefully painted and put in place, and have also fenced in the two tribal graveyards which, until now, had been roamed over by Reservation cattle,—this in addition to their usual contributions to outside mission work.

"How does Miss Kate do it?" we ask each other. How does she succeed in developing the blossom of Christian graces in soil where others find only noxious weeds of barbarism? Why do cleanliness and thrift and unselfish endeavor grow up under the weak hand of an unsupported woman rather than from beneath the strong arm of official guidance? This is a question for the guardians of the wards of the nation to answer.

Yes, Miss Kate's old root house has an attraction for us all.

Sitting out before her door one warm starlight night while we fought the ferocious mosquitoes, she spoke to us of her early trials as a missionary.

"The worst discouragement came to me through my ignorance of the language," she said. . . .

"I resolved again and again that I would give up trying to be a missionary."

"And if you had," said the Cook, as she threw away the hawthorn branch with which she had been keeping the mosquitoes at bay, and we all rose to say good night, "If you had, where would the Nez Perces be today?"

And then we left the dear Miss Kate blushing in the moonlight.

* * *

"La Grippe" has paid us a visit. For four days, Her Majesty and the medicine box were locked up together in the inner room while we all stood guard to prevent the intrusion of the Indians and their tribulations, and upon the very hour that the Allotting Agent rose weakly and sat up for breakfast, the Surveyor was laid low and James went to bed in the Photographer's dark room. Then La Grippe roamed remorselessly over the land. Many were prostrated and some died. Out of the hundred and fifty children at the school, I counted one day five girls and about twice as many boys in line for the march to dinner.

But we are all convalescent now and, in spite of the epidemic, the work has gone steadily on: and fortunately so, for there is so much to do. The utter ignorance of the Indians in the matter of land measurements and their inability to keep their boundaries in mind is discouraging. Again and again a man will come and say that he cannot find his corners, and over and over again he is shown them at the expenditure of much time, labor and patience. There has to be an end of this if the work is ever to be finished. I suspect that many will never have a true idea of the size and shape of their allotments unless Uncle Sam fences their possessions or a white man rents the land.

Nicodemus paid us a visit yesterday. He is the strongest man of the tribe and many stories are told of his wonderful feats of strength and endurance. He lives at Kamiah at the South Fork of the Clearwater and sometimes crosses the river, walking on the bottom when the water is well over his head, carrying big stones under his arms to keep him from floating.

He is having a dispute about his land boundaries with a widow whose allotment joins his own. He says he is willing to let her have her own way if he can only have peace.

* * *

An Indian has just been in to complain that the Government has given the N.P.R. [Northern Pacific Railroad] a right of way across his little farm, cutting out the very heart of it. One can forsee that before many years, under the pressure of the encroaching white man's civilization, all the valley gardens of the Nez Perces will be destroyed by the railroad lines and the Indians driven back from the water courses; and when one considers that all their little agricultural endeavors and their homes are upon these streams where alone gardens can be made, it is not difficult to conceive of the suffering which will follow this sort of opening up of the Reservation. One grows sick of seeing wrongs for which there is no practical remedy. There are plenty of *theoretical* ones, evolved in the brain of good, helpless people whose pure souls could never conceive the extent of the evils, of which they strive to devise means to trim off the outer edges—the edges which they see or hear about.

The evolution of intrinsic morality is a slow process and yet the day must come when the strong will desire to be just to the weak—if there be any weak left in that day.

Briggs says the Lion will lie down with the Lamb inside of him—when the Millennium comes upon a Reservation.

* * *

. . . But there sits Her Majesty, calmly writing, a placidity about her that is aggravating. Has she come so near the heart of the Universe that she can rest content in the stillness of the centre of it all, while I, on the outer edge, am whirled by the endless revolution into confusion of spirit with no power to listen below the noise of the mechanism?

Letter Twenty-Two

Lapwai, N.P.R.
July 10, 1891

We have been beset by many fresh difficulties this year, tangible and intangible. There is always a baleful influence at work opposing our efforts for the welfare of the Indians and interfering with the proper execution of Her Majesty's official duties. There is no difficulty in tracing this influence to its source—it is an open secret. Every Indian knows its animus and in this knowledge lies the antidote to the poison.

We cannot complain since obstructions and discouragements are brushed aside and the Allotting Agent keeps steadily on in her appointed path. Sometimes, it is true, that path has to be retraversed many times, for what has been done one day must often be all gone over again the next.

The inability of the Indians to picture the size of 160 acres of land results in the claiming by half a dozen, of a piece large enough only for one allotment. Then there are six warriors in the office and Her Majesty has to squelch five of them. And there are running fights, which go on between antagonistic temperaments, starting up anew after we think they are smothered, like the fires in the mountains.

Old Captain John and his next door neighbor, for instance. For a time, one or the other of these belligerents came daily with a complaint, and the fence between the two was moved back and forth several times. If Jonah moved it by day, Captain John set it back by night and that fence became very like the dividing line of party politics.

* * *

The 4th of July has come and gone and we still live. We are not easy to kill, but we do not rest supinely upon that fact and we do not despise the instinct of self preservation which we possess, in common with all reasoning creatures: we obey the instinct. We slept a whole week of nights with our pistol under our pillow and a man with the Cook's shot gun in the kitchen. Think of having to defend one's self against the 4th of July! But that is just what we had to do. We! Born under the shadow of Bunker Hill Monument and inoculated with Massachusetts blood!

The Nez Perce observance of the 4th of July is rather peculiar. An ancient ceremony of theirs occurred at about this season, one of the leading features of which was a general exchange of wives. In the course of time, as the tribe took on civilization, horse-racing and gambling were added to the program, together with the absorption of our national beverage; but the old leading feature was not expunged: it was simply modified in its observance to meet the approval of the Hudson Bay Company, under whose auspices the celebration of the 4th of July was initiated among the Indians.[22]

One can imagine what sort of graft the despotic, irresponsible, avaricious, Yankee-hating Englishmen who composed that company, would put upon the original celebration of our national holiday; but it is difficult to realize the effect of all this at the present time, when, as is the case, a portion of the people are struggling up toward right living and striving to get on top of their old life with all the might of awakened consciences.

In utter ignorance of the true nature of the Indian "celebration," the officials here have suffered their war processions to go on, in which naked men ride and wailing women follow, reviving old time scenes and exciting the Indians almost to frenzy,—as one man said,—"almost beyond his power to resist."

All this by day; at night,—well, we will let darkness cover the night. The girls' dormitories at this school were regularly raided, and general license prevailed among the tents of the Indian camp just outside the school enclosure. Where the carrion is, there the buzzards gather. Not a few of the white settlers of the border strayed over to celebrate their independence and ponies and blankets were lost and won on the race track with a neatness and dispatch not to be excelled at the Derby.

Last year a committee from the progressive Indians appealed to the Agent to prevent the Tal-lik-lykt (war procession), the races, and the gambling, but to no effect. The show was interesting to the white people; it was as good as a circus; the majority of the Indians wanted it; no, it must go on. And go on it did,—right through the grounds of the school; and, as the war-whoop rang out, and the women wailed, and the exploits of the braves were recited as they rode, and the scenes of the Nez Perce war,—only twelve[23] years distant,—were brought up afresh, the blood danced hotly through the Indians' veins and their wild nature mounted to the top.

"If the white people only knew how we feel," said a man who had fought in the Joseph war, and who stood by and saw Chief Joseph riding at the head of this 4th of July procession, "if they knew what these songs mean to us, there would be no more Tal-lik-lykts."

After the 4th of July had passed, and the week of racing and gambling was over, the same committee of Christian Indians waited again upon the Agent and begged him never to have this thing again. They said, "It is evil, and it hurts all."

"It is *good*," said the Agent. "It was fine, and we will have a better procession next year; and if you men interfere with my business, I'll put you in jail, and if your missionary don't stop meddling, I'll put her off the Reservation. She has put you up to this."

To which dignified language the Indians replied, "We have needed no one to tell us what is wrong; we know it ourselves," and they said no more.

This year in May these men met to consider what could be done. They dared not go to their faithful missionary for fear of bringing her into trouble. It was the third year of our presence on the Reservation. We had been weighed and tested and tried by Indian logic and Indian intuition; and it came about that the Cook stumbled upon this little troubled party in their deliberations and they told her their perplexity and their longing for help. It was pitiful. We have been ashamed of our own race often since we came among the Indians. "Christian civilization" has fallen down at our feet sometimes.

We could have stepped on it now before the "barbarism" of these men. But the Cook said that she knew that Christian civilization had not anything to do with their trouble; it had not much to do with anything on this Indian Reservation. And she looked at those silent, solemn and discouraged red men until indignation blazed from her eyes and the little group sat up straighter as she looked in their faces.

"You are men," she said. "Stand up, and don't be afraid: You have a right to appeal from your Agent to a higher authority."

"He says he will put us in jail."

"Very well, *go to jail*! That won't hurt you. It will do you good," said the Cook, "to suffer for a principle. If you are in earnest you wont mind going to jail." And they all smiled and said, "A-a-h." Then the Cook marched them off to her quarters and got a sheet of paper and then and there one— the Sunday School Superintendent—wrote a letter to the Commissioner of Indian affairs in behalf of the rest—the Elders and Deacons of the church and the whole Christian community of the Nez Perces. And the preparation for the Tal-lik-lykt went on until, about one week before the 4th, a telegram from Washington arrived, forbidding the war procession, horse-racing and gambling in the *vicinity of the school*.

It was like the bursting of a bomb-shell at the Agency. There was hurrying to and fro; councils and indignation meetings were held at night up and down in the tribe. The Agent was sorry for the disappointed ones and said so. He "doubted if the Commissioner had a right to forbid racing: it was done all over the country. The President himself would not turn his back upon a good match of horses. White people went to horse races; why deprive the Indians of the innocent pleasure?" And the tewats, the sorcerers of the tribe, rode past the cabin of the missionary, crying out, "Now you must go! Agent says now you must go!" The innocent woman got the blame. She was the marplot and the guilty Cook escaped, as she generally did, the consequences of her rash deeds.

There was no war procession; but a race track was marked out on the uplands and for a whole week the ponies galloped and the blankets were staked and lost and won, and just outside the school fence the camp was pitched. Hence the pistol and shot-gun in our establishment and the armed watch at the dormitories. It is but justice to the Superintendent of the school to relate that, when informed of the true nature of the Tal-lik-lykt, he took instant and active measures, as far as lay in his power, to suppress it. He it was who supplemented the Cook's shot-gun and our pistol with fire-arms for all his employees and stood guard himself all night, for a whole week of nights, until the camp was broken up. But as he had caused the crier to proclaim, on the first day, that any Indian caught within the school enclosure after dark would be shot without warning, the moral influence of our weapons was all that was required.

Thus a great step has been taken in the right direction. Hence forth there will be two parties in the tribe and a spirited fight will go on. If the powers that be, the officials of the Government, could but cast their influence upon the right side, the battle would not be for long. [24]

We have been out to camp but once so far this season, and then we did not really camp. We pitched our tent; but the rattlesnakes were too numerous on the spot and Her Majesty, though she would defy Lucifer himself in the line of her duty, said it was foolish to needlessly jump a rattlesnake claim. So we retired into the cabin of a white settler and fought the bloodthirsty *cimex lectularius* [bedbug], whose name was legion, all night. On the third night the Cook expressed her preference for a fair fight with an honorable rattlesnake, and hereafter, we shall take our chances with the indigenous fauna of the country.

Our Surveyor is running out the lines in the unsurveyed portions of the Reservation. He comes upon queer things in distant and out-of-the-way places, and the mild-natured man is growing fierce in indignation. Now it is a big timber steal, whereby the Indians are defrauded of thousands of dollars; then it is a water steal, whereby the streams are diverted by white men's ditches and Indian gardens left dry and barren; and all the time it is a pasture steal, whereby Indian cattle are crowded from their fields and the increase taken from them by the greedy border settler, the irresponsible stockmen, who want the earth and are going to get it.

* * *

. . . Last year, we were in Kamiah on the 4th of July and were invited to the celebration by the Nez Perces of that locality, and we went, glad to be counted in among the simple people. It was an all day affair, ushered in by the meeting, at the church, of the whole community, for many miles around; big and little, ponies, dogs and babies; and a happier set of creatures I never saw. They formed a procession, headed by the Sunday School children and marched in and out among the pine trees up to the church, singing something which we could not understand, the refrain only being intelligible; "Hurrah! 4th July! Hurrah! 4th July!" Then there were speeches and songs galore, and the native pastor blessed the people, after which there was a great scurrying to make ready the barbecue and the feast.

The work seemed to have been perfectly planned.

There were men appointed to make the fires and bring wood and water, and women to prepare the meat and fish and others to cook it. Great strips of beef were strung on poles before the fire and salmon stretched over the glowing coals and pots of soup hung above the blaze; and all to the accompaniment of merry laughter and cheerful chatter.

Tents had been pitched the day before, each family bringing its own, and there was a large one in which all the people gathered for meetings three times during the day. Clothes were stretched upon the grass and tables prepared, each family having brought its own dishes and contributed to the food supply. The people were served by the elders and deacons of the church, the old people first, the children last.

Elder Felix selected a specially choice bit from the toasting salmon for Her Majesty and not until the last one of the great company had left the table, did he and his fellow servers submit to be waited upon. When the feast was over, Her Majesty was asked to speak to the people and there I am afraid that pestilential Declaration of Independence came upon the scene again, and was explained and the meaning of the 4th of July set forth in James' most stirring Nez Perce.

You would have said that there were a very patriotic crowd that day, could you have heard the "Aah's" and the cheers which followed James' interpretation. There is a good deal of oratorical ability about James. I have always suspected that Her Majesty's ordinary business transactions were heavily ornamented with rhetorical embroidery; but here was a strictly legitimate opportunity and James improved it.

In a subsequent conversation with the Cook he admitted improvising somewhat upon a few points ommitted by Her Majesty. At all events, the speech was a success and gave great pleasure to the old, as well as the young, Nez Perces. Our part in the day's doings ended with a Council held to decide upon the adoption into the tribe of several Indians who wished to be allotted. They had long lived with the tribe and had no other home. That matter being settled, the old men were asked to listen to the reading of the list of allotments so far as it was finished and to approve the work. It was interesting to note the care with which each name was considered and the readiness to supply any omission, or correct an inadvertent error. If a child had been born since a family had been registered, there was solicitude to have it counted in, or, if there had been a death, the desire was unanimously expressed to have the allotment stand for the benefit of the next of kin. There was no dissension in the council on that 4th of July, for all the malcontents had gone to Lapwai, and when we left the ground to go to our little cabin, we were followed by good wishes and pleasant words from all. As we sat upon our door steps and listened to the evening hymns and watched the camp fires burn low and go out and the tents disappear in the nightfall, how could we but be satisfied with the Kamians, and how could we help travelling, in thought, up the trail to Mount Idaho to thank the lonely little woman, to whose influence with her red children the right inception of the allotment was so much in-debted.

The Photographer tried to get a picture of the people as they sat on the yellow grass in the glare of the mid-day sun, but it came out painfully hard and contrasts. Photography in a semi-arid country is not a cheerful occupation at the best, when one considers the water required in the process and the fact that one often is obliged to take one's own bath in a pint of the precious liquid.

Letter Twenty-Three

LAPWAI
August 15th, 1891

* * *

One cannot be with Her Majesty day after day and month after month without imbibing something of her scientific spirit. The Photographer, even, has become charged with the energy of archaeological research. The anthropometric mania has reached us, a requisition being made upon Her Majesty for some measurements to help out the World's Fair Exhibits.[25] The instruments were handed over to the Photographer as having most spare time to devote to this nascent science. But the Photographer, chiefly theoretical in his spare hours, suggested that the practical Cook should make the first trial upon James.

James was brought in and planted against the wall, and the Cook took his height, the size of his head, his width, length of his nose, shape of his ears, color of his hair and eyes; in fact, every item in the book of instructions, except the expansion of his chest and shoulders, for the calipers sent for that purpose could stretch only eleven inches. The Photographer lost his interest at this discovery. "Of course, we can't go on," said he.

The Cook mildly inquired what his head was made for if it could not help him out of a small difficulty like that.

"We must *make* a pair of calipers," said she and we all began to pass in review the resources of the locality for material of construction. Briggs suggested a pair of steer's horns, but the Photographer was satisfied to sit down between the horns of the dilemna, as if his responsibility in the matter was at an end. His was a receptive character, easily affected by his environment. He exhibited but a languid interest when the Cook exclaimed, "I have it! The 'arch of triumph' will be just the thing!"

Now the arch of triumph was the back of the Photographer's chair and it had just the right curve. The Cook instructed James to bisect it, shave it down flat, bolt the two straight ends together, and sharpen the curved ends to a fine point. In an incredibly short time the calipers were in fine working order and James was measured all over again and the result recorded in one of the blanks furnished for the purpose.

James was measured several more times, in the presence of various other Indians as an object lesson, in the attempt to excite their interest and cooperation in the work, but to no purpose. They evidently thought these mysterious instruments were some white man's contrivance to cheat them out of their remaining possessions—their ears and their eyes. Some, perhaps, imagined the performance a piece of necromancy which might result in the laming of their horses. If James had met with any misfortune within a year, it would have been traced to those calipers, such is the way some people's minds work. . . .

We tried to catch the school children, but at the first sight of those fearful calipers, they took to flight and, we really not having the time to be scientific, the anthropometric tools were turned over to the school superintendent who had the authority to compel, and the children grew to like the operation after they found it did not hurt their feelings half as much as a lesson in arithmetic.

But her little experiments left the Cook with a puzzle on her mind. She had, when her attention had been drawn to the matter, found the Nez Perce heads rather large, and there was nothing in her experience that could account for the fact. It surely could not require much room to hold one idea at a time; the heads must be solid.

The unsolved problem rankled in her mind and absorbed her attention so much that she failed to perceive that the Photographer was acting in a strange manner. He took long walks and was reported as being seen in out-of-the-way places, and he was preoccupied at meal time. Little the Cook guessed that he, too, was wrestling with her problem. The anthropological germ had found a lodgment in both, and one day it all came out. The Photographer said he had noticed some queer depressions in the earth not far from our cabin and he thought it would be a good plan to excavate one; it might prove an ancient grave with a skull in it.

"Her Majesty particularly wants some Nez Perce crania," said the Cook, disguising her own thirst for knowledge on the subject. "Yes," said the Photographer, "I heard her say she would like to have some crania for the Peabody Museum."

"We will start this very afternoon," said the enthusiastic cook, and so, as soon as the Allotting Agent was absorbed in her work and would not notice their absence, they armed themselves with all the implements in the camp, an axe, a fire shovel, and a big spoon. There was a spade, but it could not be found, and they set off in a state of high expectancy. They found the depressions, each one covered with a heap of stones. Selecting one of the largest mounds, the Photographer proceeded to remove the stones and, when that was accomplished, he looked at his hands, and sighed, and sat down to rest, while the Cook, with the axe, marked the outline of the excavation they were to make. Then she stood at rest looking at the Photographer. He was humming "The Better Land" and his eyes had a far away look.

"I think we have done enough for one day," said he. "I want to take a picture of the locality before we go any farther. Her Majesty says *that* is important."

"Perhaps you had better pile up the stones again if you want to get a picture of the undisturbed condition."

"Oh, no! that is not necessary," and he got up stiffly and walked limpingly away, leaving the deserted Cook to make up her mind for the thousandth time, not to depend upon a partnership for success in any undertaking.

She began to dig, she worked rapidly until the fire shovel bent and broke in her hands then she took the big iron spoon, which, though inadequate, was like herself, unyielding under pressure. She scraped and scooped and her enthusiasm grew. She forgot the personal interest she had in finding Nez Perce crania; the ethnological fever was in her brain and she was working in the interest of pure science alone. To be sure, she would like to spring a triumph upon Her Majesty, who had, she knew, small faith in the value of lay explorations. She would like to show her that the labors of amateurs, outside of culinary operations, were sometimes productive of results which commanded respect. She bent to her task and the big iron spoon shone brighter and brighter and brighter for its unwonted use. An Indian passed down the trail beside her and paused to look, but he asked no questions: he only wondered what sort of root she was grubbing for in that stony ground. She dug on with the energy of a coyote, until she came upon red earth mixed with bits of charcoal.

"The Nez Perces burned their dead," said she in a high state of excitement. Then she came upon some snail shells, and her excitement grew. She was so absorbed in her work that she had not noticed that rain was falling. Great drops now splashed into the excavation and her back was growing damp. She decided to return to camp and find an umbrella. She took a handful of snail shells and charcoal and presented herself before Her Majesty.

"I found these," she said, "in one of those depressions under the stones."

"How far below the surface?" asked Her Majesty magisterially.

"Eighteen inches, and the shells also."

"They are probably intrusive," said Her Majesty.

"Most things on the Reservation *are*!" replied the Cook.

There was no speculation in the Allotting Agent's eye; she calmly went on with her writing and the Cook began to discount her find and to feel the chill of her wet shoulders.

"You had better take James and a shovel," said Her Majesty, as the Cook, having found an umbrella, went out again.

James was found sleeping under a tree and was persuaded to accompany the Cook. Now James was not blinded by ethnological zeal or, indeed, enthusiasm of any color, and it is natural that a man's theories should harmonize with the dominant part of his nature. James had his theory,—the Cook's excavation was not a point of departure for the Nez Perce soul. It was a cooking range, where the aborigine had roasted his camas, and he explained the modus operandi.

"They dig a hole," said he, "and line it with hot stones, place the camas on the stones, cover up the hole with grass and earth and let it steam for two or three days," and he smacked his lips in blissful memory of the good old times.

The Cook was disappointed, though glad to have come at the truth. However, she was not dangerous in her disappointment as some scientific people are; she had never advocated vivisection, and there was no fear of her killing an Indian to substantiate her theory.

She had already every proof of the solidarity of the crania except that of ocular demonstration. Here, for instance, was Her Majesty,—had she not endeavored for two years to beat a certain idea into the Indian's head and it had only flattened on the outside and added a new layer of impenetrability. The Department should have furnished Her Majesty with a cold chisel and sledge hammer, if they expected her to teach surveying to the average Indian.

There was an old chief here today, asking her to make the Surveyor put his corners where he, the chief, wanted them. The idea that the lines must run north, and south, and east, and west, has not yet penetrated his skull.

"It is no use to try to prematurely develop anything," says the Cook, and now she reasons that a great thickness of skull may be a wise provision of nature,—to protect the dawning intelligence in the infancy of the race. If it was hard to get an idea into the aboriginal head, it was just as hard to get one out, and she had noticed, since she came West, that the process of losing was much more rapid and certain than that of gaining. That the Indian had succeeded in preserving so much of the original uprightness to which he had attained before the advent of the white race upon his territory, might be owing to the thickness of the occiput,—she would not question the wisdom of nature.

The only regrettable outcome of this ethnological flurry was the coolness which remained between the Photographer and the Cook. The one had, within the last two years, developed a habit of sitting down under difficulties which the other resented.

But the Cook has now a well founded belief that there are no ancient receptacles of the dead on the Nez Perce Reservation. She thinks that graves are modern, introduced by the pioneer missionaries who insisted then,—as they do now,—that their converts should prove their sincerity by altering their habits and customs, good and bad, to conform to the ideas and practices of another race. . . .

Letter Twenty-Four

Lapwai
August 15th, 1891

. . . We have been out this morning on the Genesee road and as we were driving up from the ferry, we met a wagon load of children with a white man and an Indian woman on the seat in front. We took no special notice of the rather unusual circumstance, but when we passed a second and a third wagon, we said, "There must be a circus in Lewiston." And then it came out that Her Majesty had let it be known that when white men came to have their children allotted it would be well to bring a marriage certificate with their application, and these wagon loads were going to Lewiston for that certificate. Why the children were taken did not appear plain to us but evidently through some idea that their presence might be necessary to the performance of the ceremony which was to furnish the certificate.

The men bowed cordially and Her Majesty beamed approvingly upon them and the women smiled and the children looked as if they were, indeed, going to a circus. These "squaw men" have generous impulses. They had no use for a marriage certificate, but they were willing to accommodate Her Majesty at so trifling an expense.

* * *

Old Billy is now at Lapwai. He has come to talk with Her Majesty about the old times of his people; and he is making a map for her, to show the location of the various Nez Perce bands or villages, the water courses and trails, and other topographical features of the country. He gives the original names of the villages, their significance, and a little history of each band, their characteristics and political relation to each other.[26]

Such a band controlled such other bands; these could not hunt in such a direction without the permission of that, and so on. You see that the old man has set himself quite a task, with nothing but his memory to draw upon. So far, he has nearly a hundred villages upon his map and he is beginning to look very tired. He says he cannot sleep with thinking of the old days.

The Photographer has taken a snap at Billy as he sat resting at Miss Kate's door. I wish I could also send you the map to look at, but it is too precious. It must go to the Museum for safe keeping.

The coat Billy has on is one he cut and made himself out of a blanket.

* * *

Miss Kate is becoming interested in Her Majesty's anthropological researches. She sees now that she has had, in the Nez Perce tribe, unsuspected opportunities of increasing the world's knowledge in this line.

Like the great majority of missionaries she has bent her

energies to the obliteration of old customs and beliefs, class-ing them as heathen. She is beginning to see that there is more in the old Indian philosophy than she ever dreamed of and that there might have been something of value saved if she had known how.

Old blind Abraham has told her about the peace pipes or calumets. He says they were much used in old times, but that their significance has been almost lost since the advent of the white race among the people, the young Nez Perces not knowing what their ornamentation stood for.

* * *

About the middle of July, we were all invited to Felix's wedding. The mercury stood at 115°, but we had assisted at the burial of his former wife and he was anxious to have our approbation of this, his second choice.

She is a sister of Chief Joseph, a comely and wise woman who will be a true help-meet and they will surely be a happy couple if they but fulfill the obligations taken upon them-selves at the marriage ceremony. As James interpreted it, Fe-lix promised not to strike with his hand or his foot and she, not to strike with her tongue.

Her Majesty has reminded us that it is not so very long ago that the law had to regulate, for our own race, the di-mensions of the stick the husband might use in chastising his wife. It could not exceed the thickness of his thumb.

Felix has been made an Indian Judge and he wants a copy of the laws of Idaho. Her Majesty has promised to obtain one for him.

He has a daughter who can read and he wants to learn how to do justice in his new position. Good for Felix! He has grown a great deal since the discomfiture of Tobias and San-ballat at the rebuilding of Kamiah church. It is quite as much the grip of superstitious fear of the old chiefs' power as the bewildering over mastery of the white race, that benumbs the Indian's faculties.

* * *

. . . It is cold weather now, but the children were running about in calico garments, for you see the school is a Govern-ment boarding school, where the guardians of the Indians furnish everything out of the money belonging to their wards and, as there are three thousand miles between the great guardians and the little children, accidents will happen now and then.

The Superintendent seemed sorry about the calico dresses; he also said that shoes for about one third of the children had come, but, so far, no flannel or blankets. There were stockings enough, but they were mostly men's sizes and he pointed to a group of boys who were reciting a spelling lesson, and I saw the big heels of their stockings sticking up over the top of their shoes.

But the room was packed full of eager children, bright as weasels. When recess time came, they clung about Mr. McConville so closely that he could hardly move. Three little girls took hold of his hands, a boy climbed on a chair to stroke his face and three others looked as if they were going to climb on his back.

"Run away now and play," said he, and the boys, grabbing their caps, skipped off to play leap frog and the girls to make tents for their dollies.

The teacher told me that the children were very easy to manage: that it was not natural for them to tell falsehoods; that they did it so awkwardly that they were found out at once. They sang a pretty little song for me, but I could not hear what it was about for the Nez Perce tongue does not get round our language very well. The teacher said that the whole eighty of them sang together every night "Now I lay me down to sleep" and they marched off, two by two, to bed and were snugly tucked in with the cotton sheet which was the coverlet.

Many of the fathers and mothers of these children live in tents summer and winter, making their bed on the ground where they keep nice and warm in blankets and furs; but they do not have much to eat so Uncle Sam, the great guardian, takes the children away for fear they may starve, or not have their hair cut properly and should wear moccasins instead of shoes and stockings and should grow up without being able to read the newspapers which they never see or count the money they never have. It is best to be prepared, though, for some time these little boys and girls may be free to go where newspapers and books grow and money can be had for the earning of it. Her Majesty is making up a party now to take to Carlisle when we leave this place. A great many of the children tease to go but the Agent thinks it better for them to stay at home: that "an Indian has a better chance to become a white man on the Reservation than in Pennsylvania." But there are white men and white men just as there are many kinds of Indians and I have noticed that when we teach *our* children to write we set them a nice fair "copy," straight and clean, with a pretty sentiment in it or a bit of poetry. We do not set dirty, crooked, blotted lines of swear words for them to imitate.

Mr. McConville, the school superintendent, would be very glad to send all his little brown children away while they are yet clean and pure in heart so they could grow up white inside, if they did have to be darker in skin than their little brothers and sisters in Pennsylvania. . . .

The other day, as I was strolling along Lapwai creek near its junction with the Clearwater, I stumbled upon a stone lying half hidden in the grass. It was round, with a square hole in the centre out of which a little plant was growing and I knew that it was a mill stone, but how came it there? . . .

The story of that stone I am going to tell you in a round-about way just as Old Billy and Miss Kate told it to me, with a preface to make it clear because, as your wise Aunt says, we must always go from the known to the unknown to get a right understanding of a subject.

Well, you know that there once lived in this country a man by the name of Thomas Jefferson. He was a man that ideas were apt to come to when they were ready to set the world off on a new track. The particular idea that came to Mr. Jefferson at the end of the eighteenth century (1792) was that the great unexplored land west of the Missouri River might be worth looking into. . . .

Mr. Jefferson, being President of the United States, sent his own private Secretary, Captain Lewis, to command the expedition, and he was accompanied by Captain William Clark. We cannot follow the party very closely, but sometime you will read the Lewis and Clark journals which are very interesting. The men were fitted out by the Government with horses and everything they needed for the long journey, even with guns to kill game and Indians as they went along.

I think Lewis and Clark were wise men and not so fond of killing as many explorers are. They met many tribes of Indians and pretty generally avoided having any trouble with them. Indians gave them food and horses and in return received guns and knives and trinkets: often they divided their last morsel freely with the travellers who were often hungry, sometimes being obliged to kill and eat their horses.

On the 20th of September 1805, when the men had become weak and thin and many were ill, they "descended the last of the Rocky Mountains and reached the level country," a beautiful open plain with trees scattered over it. And there they saw three Indian boys who ran away and hid in the grass. They were Nez Perce boys and when they had carried the news of the arrival of the white men home, a man came out to meet Lewis and Clark and led the travellers to the Nez Perce village; and right here I must tell you what a mistake was made about the name of this tribe.

It is never easy to come at the name of an Indian or even of an Indian tribe. A tribe has always at least two names; one they call themselves by and one by which they are known to other tribes. All the tribes living west of the Rocky Mountains were called "chupnit-pa-lu" by the people who lived east of the mountains. "Chupnit-pa-lu" means *people of the pierced noses*; it also means *emerging from the bushes* or *forest*; the *people from the woods*.

The tribes on the Columbia river used to pierce the nose and wear in it some ornament as you have seen some old fashioned white ladies in their ears. Lewis and Clark had with them an interpreter whose wife was a Shoshone or Snake woman and so it came about that when it was asked "What Indians are these?" the answer was "They are 'Chupnit-pa-lu'" and it was written down in the journal; spelled rather queerly, for white people's ears do not always catch Indian tones and of course the Indians could not spell any word.

It was written "Chopunnish." Chopunnish is not much like Chupnit-pa-lu and it is not known in the Nez Perce tribe: the oldest man never heard of it. Old Billy says, "We have a name that does not belong to us. We are not pierced noses and never were. We are the 'Nemapo.' When Lewis and Clark came into our country they were very hungry and their horses were all bones."

"They were the first white men that many of the people had ever seen and the women thought them beautiful." Billy's grandfather shook hands with the strangers and talked with them in the sign language and all the chiefs were sent for to welcome the little company of white men and to find out what could be done to help them. The Journal says that the Nez Perces were kind to the tired and hungry party. They furnished fresh horses and dried meat and fish with wild po-tatoes and other roots which were good to eat, and the re-freshed white men went further on, westward, leaving their bony, wornout horses for the Indians to take care of and have fat and strong when Lewis and Clark should come back on their way home.

It was in the early spring, in May, when they returned. The weather was cold, with snow on the high lands and mud in the villages, and they were again hungry and worn with hard travel and want of proper food. The Nez Perces went out to meet them and brought the whole party down into Kamiah (which Lewis and Clark spell Commearp) and there they set up a large leathern tent which the Chief said was for their home as long as they wished to stay among the Indians: and there they lived a whole month, like brothers with the Nez Perces. The people brought roots and dried salmon and the Journal says that "not being accustomed to live on roots alone, we feared that such food might make our men sick and therefore proposed to exchange one of our good horses, which was rather poor, for one that was fatter which we might kill.

"The hospitality of the Chiefs was offended at the idea of an exchange. He observed that his people had an abundance of young horses and that if we were disposed to use that food, we might have as many as we wanted."

It is very interesting to read what Lewis and Clark write about their friendly camping in the Kamiah valley, but it really does not belong to the story. These white men learned something of the Nez Perce language, enough to convey some new ideas to the Indians: not very clearly but sufficiently well to set them thinking. The new ideas were about God, a great Being that every race and tribe are always trying to know something about. The Nez Perces had been trying all their lives. Old Billy said no matter how hard they tried "it was all fog," and that after Lewis and Clark came they doubted more and more their old ways of worship.

Then the Hudson Bay traders came,—King George men, they were called,—and the people began to worship the Sun and he, Billy, remembered dancing around the sun pole which was set up near the present site of Walla Walla.[27] But still the people were not satisfied and as year after year passed by, they held councils to talk about their trouble, always ending with "If we could only find the path of Lewis and Clark, and follow it, we would find the light."

So the little imperfect idea grew and grew until, twenty-five years after the Jefferson exploring party had gone away from the "Choupnit people," these Indians, groping in the dark, determined to send a delegation to find Lewis and Clark and learn the truth: they could not live in the dark any longer. The idea had grown so imperative that it must be satisfied with knowledge.

Four men were chosen. Billy gave their names as

Tip-ya-lah-na-jek-nin, (Black or Speaking Eagle), a chief, was Kip's grandfather. He had seen Lewis and Clark and received a medal from them.

Ka-on-pu, (Man of the Morning or Daylight), an old man. His mother was a Flathead, his father a Nez Perce.

Hi-youts-tihan (Rabbits Skin Legging) was Black Eagle's mother's son, a young man of the same band as Yellow Bull, whom we know.

Tawis-sis-sin-nin (Little Horns or No Horns). He was Billy's father's sister's son, a young man about twenty years of age.[28]

Billy was about ten years old when these four men

started. They went out on the Lolo trail, the same that Lewis and Clark had come on.

They did not know where to go and they had no pillar of cloud to lead them by day or a star to follow by night.

They were led only by their hopes and urged on by their lorging. Billy described the hopeful starting when all the people went out to see them well on the way and "stood watching till they were out of sight, and not any more dust rose against the sky"—then the patient waiting for the long delayed return and, at last,—the woe and despair of the stricken people.

There had been many councils of the old men of the tribe about this journey. Some way, no one knew how, word had come to the Nez Perces that Captain Clark was in St. Louis and the delegation of four were bidden to find their way to that city. They were to see Captain Clark and ask him to tell them about the truth, the light. Some people have said that they went in search of a book, the Bible, but when I asked Billy about this, he said no, they went to find Lewis and Clark and learn about the better way to worship God. The people were poor and miserable and often hungry and they knew not where to look for help in their trouble and they were sure that Lewis and Clark could tell them. There was nothing so definite in their minds as a book, and that makes this wonderful journey more wonderful still.

The Nez Perces were just children crying in the night and reaching out to touch the Mother, who was close beside them though they knew it not.

Old Billy could tell me nothing of the four men after they went out of sight over the Kamian hills, but we learn something of them from other sources. They arrived in St. Louis sometime in May or June, 1831, four travel stained red men asking for Lewis and Clark. Clark was then Superintendent of Indian affairs for the Northwest, and the Indians met him and explained, as best they could, their mission.

It does not appear that they received much comfort: there was the barrier of language and the indefiniteness of their object: the crying in the night could not be translated. The men hung around the office of the Indian Agent day after day, silent and sad.

"Who are they?" the people would ask. "Where do they come from?" A fur trader, a Frenchman, seeing them, said, "I know who they are. They come from West of the Rocky Mountains. They are Chup-nit-pa-lu." only he translated the word into his own language—"They are the Nez Perce," said he.

"To make a long story short, the two oldest Indians sickened and died in St. Louis, and the two younger started back upon a steamboat, on the Yellowstone River. Near the mouth of the river Old Billy's cousin died and Hi-youts-tihan, the last of the four, never came back to his people. He could not see their faces when they knew how it had fared with their messengers. Some Nez Perces met and talked with him in Montana and learned that the white people had promised to send a teacher to the Nez Perces, and so they waited and waited until at last, in 1838, the teacher came. His name was Henry Spalding and he brought his wife with him over the mountains and they were father and mother to their Indian children.

I saw Mr. Spalding in Washington, after he had grown old, and he gave me his photograph. He spent thirty years with the Nez Perces and taught them many things which are still remembered in the tribe.

And this brings me to that old mill stone, lying in the grass. The Indians made gardens under the instruction of Mr. and Mrs. Spalding and cultivated wheat and barley and raised vegetables and fruit and they found a "proper stone" and hammered it into shape and Mr. Spalding showed them how to make a mill to grind their grain and this is the very same old stone.

The mill has gone to pieces and Mr. Spalding's house is now used by an Agency Indian, Jim Moses, to keep his horses in, for the Government sends Agents instead of Missionaries now, to teach the Indians. . . .

* * *

Letter Twenty-Five

LAPWAI
November 27th, 1891

We have made a fresh camp every few days this year, being pressed on all sides by the Indians who are now clamorous for speedy allotting and there seems to be no end to them. Their movements are probably hastened by an order issued by the Department that no Indian can go hunting until he has been allotted. The tribe has its ramifications through the neighboring tribes and the mixed bloods are now claiming Nez Perce inheritance. They are entitled to an allotment somewhere, only Her Majesty must take care that they do not get it in more than one place; two allotments, in fact. This makes much letter writing, in correspondence with the officials of the tribes represented by the applicants, and oh, the time it takes! . . .

Wati-Wati-Houlis had been with us for several weeks as extra camp man. When he came, he brought his wife and child and they pitched their tent not far from our own. It was pleasant, when, in the morning, we drew aside our door flap, to see Wati's tent all in order, thrown open to the air and sun, and Lily playing beside her Mother who sat on a mat, sewing and crooning softly to the child. It was a picture of peace and contentment.

Wati was a faithful worker and the Cook never wanted for help in her peculiar trials while he was with us. When we returned from the field there was always a bright fire burning on a sort of stove altar built so that the Cook need not stoop over her duties and the little child was a pretty diversion.

She was only about three years old and yet in our various movings she rode a "gentle horse" named Jonah, sometimes thirty miles a day, and seemed to thrive on it. Her father used to tie her, in some complicated manner, upon the horse so that she was both comfortable and safe. Then she would toss the bridle and prattle to Jonah who evidently understood her small talk and responded to it by his ears, which language Lily perfectly comprehended. They were great friends, the baby and the animal, and the old horse never stumbled with his precious load.

When the Photographer took a snap at our camp, Jonah and Lily were in the foreground and not long afterwards Wati left us for some more profitable employment and we lost sight of the family until lately, since our return to Lapwai. One cold morning the man and his wife came to see us. They looked old and worn and when we enquired for Lily the Mother said she was dead and that they had come over the mountains to ask us for that photograph.

The desolated parents sat down on the door steps of our quarters and told us their pitiful story. The Photographer gave the picture and, miserable as it was, they caressed it as if it had been the child herself. They talked to it and cried over it and finally the mother wrapped it carefully in a bit of paper and hid it in the bosom of her dress. The Cook sat dumb beside them but Her Majesty found comforting words to speak and they rode away quietly, believing that they had not forever lost their only child, and repeating "Aah! Aah!" to the last words of Her Majesty.

We moved from Camp Lily on the 10th of October. . . . Our new camp was at the junction of the road to Kamiah and that which led to Pierce City. There was no fuel, but water was to be had in a bog close by. The vicinity was camping ground for travellers to the mines and we were often wakened at early dawn by the sounds from a camp we could not see.

Sometimes it was a group of rough miners swearing at their pack mules, but oftener it was the morning hymn of a band of Christian Indians who had halted for the night on their way to Pierce City with a train of provisions for the mines.

There would be women and children in the party each with some part of the work to do. We always liked to lie still while the stars were fading above our tent and listen to the tones of the Father's prayer, wafted to us on the gentle breeze of the dawn: and the queer twisted hymn of our Kamian friends which we could hardly recognize as "Awake my soul and with the sun" always came to us fraught with a blessing. Then, when we knew that the party had breakfasted, we would go out to exchange a few pleasant words while the packs were being roped on the ponies, the Cook studying the mysterious diamond hitch while Her Majesty chatted in dreadfully broken Nez Perce. . . .

We have had a sure enough Thanksgiving dinner. Briggs and Miss Kate assisted at that dinner. Our Menu was not very elaborate but there was a turkey, pumpkin pie, plum pudding and some little fixings besides. The plum pudding came from Chicago, the soup from Pittsburgh, the pumpkin from Boston; the turkey was indigenous to the country. . . .

Letter Twenty-Six

LAPWAI
June 8th, 1892

The Allotting Agent has a secret from the Cook; she has guarded it effectually. . . . A paper has been lying on the office table, upon which, from time to time, Her Majesty makes a few notes in an abstracted sort of way, as if there were some heavy weight upon her official conscience, some pronounced inertia at the point of her pen.

. . . It was cool and cloudy, and there was an air of resignation about the Special Agent as she sat down at the table and placed the apparently important paper before her, and dipped her pen in the ink. At this critical moment there was a knock at the door and three Indians entered the room. They were old men of pure, unadulterated North American pedi-

154

Resolving a dispute over ownership of an allotment. Alice Fletcher and James Stuart at left *(Idaho Historical Society)*

"Clearwater River—Nicodemus' home on the left" (*Idaho Historical Society*)

Camp with Briggs and his wife *(Idaho Historical Society)*

"Old Billy Williams" *(Idaho Historical Society)*

"Nez Perce Woman's Industrial Society." Kate McBeth in back row, right (*Schlesinger Library, Radcliffe College*)

Lapwai schoolgirls *(Idaho Historical Society)*

"Consultations on land allotment." Alice Fletcher in shelter, Charley Adams at left, Louise Kipp at right *(Idaho Historical Society)*

Greer's Ferry. Looking down on the Clearwater River (*Idaho Historical Society*)

gree, men whose word was as good as a white man's bond. They beamed upon Her Majesty—they had come to welcome her on her return from the East.

"We were afraid not to see you again," they said.

"And why were you afraid?"

"Agent told the Indians you would never come back; that Washington would send out a new Allotting Agent to do the work all over."

"He said," explained the youngest of the three men, "that you had been cutting the land into little three-cornered pieces, and it would not stand."

"He said that the Indians would see that *he* had the power; that nobody had any say about things on the Reservation but *him* and that the Indians who believed in you would get into trouble," remarked the oldest of the three.

"Well," replied Her Majesty, "I am here to finish the work."

"And now we have a good heart," said the Indians, "but when you go away it is all buzz-buzz, all talk-talk, and we are tired. We want to go on our land, but if the allotment won't stand it is all bad."

"*Go* on your land," said the Cook, who was always holding up to the Indians' view the advantages of what she called "back-bone." "Go on your land, and *stay* there."

"Aah," said the three men as they shook hands and filed out and Her Majesty took up her pen, and re-adjusted the paper before her.

Tat-tat-tat at the door and in walked Techoke. Now Techoke was half Nez Perce and half French. He had been born and brought up on the Reservation and belonged to a large and influential family. He had been a chief and was a progressive, intelligent man, with the stability of the Indian joined to the courtesy of the Frenchman.

"What you say 'bout this half-breed trouble, Mees," asked he, after the usual hearty greeting. "We bin go on our land. Agent say we have no rights here, half-breeds no land. Nez Perce mother not count, what you say? I tell Indians say nothing, wait till 'The Woman' come."

"Is your land fenced, Techoke?"

"Yes, all fenced, and all plow."

"Very well, I do not think it can be taken from you," and then followed an hour's explanation of the Assistant Attorney General's decision in the case of Jane Waldron, and its bearings upon the titles to real estate in general, and Indian lands in particular, to all of which Techoke, who had recently been elected Judge, listened attentively.

"Agent frighten people much," said he. "I tell them what you say." By the time Techoke had gone, the spring had gone out of the Alloting Agent. She feebly lifted her pen, and after a moment's reflection, wrote a line and a half, when there was a muffled tread of moccasined feet on the porch and Teusah and Tono opened the door of the office. Young Indians they, who are raising watermelons and potatoes and children on this side of the Clearwater, where they have each built a snug little frame house, with the bulk of their allotments across the river. They had been filled with the idea of being citizens in the future. They had no horses fit to plow with and only one pair of hands apiece. They hit upon the scheme of hiring Norwegians to break their fields. They got out the posts, and furnished the wire, and hired the Norwegians, who had teams, and were neighbors just over the line, to plow and put in a crop of wheat. They reasoned that in a few years they would accumulate enough to go alone. They were hopeful when we left last November; they came to ask a few questions now which had grown up in the vista of citizenship.

"Are the babies all well, Tono?" asked the Cook.

"Yes, Sir." (From some undefined mutual obliquity, Tono always said "sir" to the Cook.) "Yes, Sir, all well." Then Teusah broke out with "Do Citizens have Agents over them?"

"No."

"Is a man a citizen whose father was white?"

"If the father was a citizen the children are born free," replied the Special Agent.

Evidently Teusah had been doing a good deal of thinking. His face lightened all over as he said, "Then I am already a citizen."

"Yes, Teusah, you are a citizen."

Tono, whose skin was a shade darker, looked less hopeful. "What is the good of an agent any how to us," he asked. "The Nez Perces can take care of themselves."

"Tono," said Her Majesty, "what is in your mind?"

"Last year," answered the big boy, "you told us to work hard on our land, and bimeby we be rich men and citizens. We talk it over, Teusah and me, and we pay white men to help us. Agent last winter, after you go away, *orders* white men off and tell us to stop work on that land; Washington said so: what we go to do now? Too much trouble 'bout that land, guess I not want to be citizen."

"Oh, yes, you do," interrupted the Cook. "You will have a vote, and votes help a great deal, Tono."

Tono looked dazed. Perhaps he was making a mental estimate of how much they paid over in Moscow for a vote, and whether, after all, the privilege did not cost more than it was worth.

The Special Agent was making little scratches on that mysterious paper: little rings and squares and figure eights. The Cook notices that she makes no straight lines. All the diagrams are *closed*. There was no way out of them. She seemed absorbed and hardly noticed when Teusah and Tono went out.

The Cook invited the pair to call again to talk about their affairs, but there was little response. Somehow their enthusiasm had been dampened in our absence. It was afternoon by this time and the Cook went to brew a cup of beef tea for Her Majesty. On her return, she found Tse-kol and Pah-los in the room. Tse-kol is a Christian Indian of the old Presbyterian type, is a hard worker and wants very much to be a citizen: believes in it as he does in what he knows of the Westminster Catechism, with all the strength that is in him. He is trying to earn money so as properly to adorn his citizenship when it comes. Great is his faith. He has the contract to furnish the Lapwai school with fuel. He has cut the wood on the mountains and comes to ask help for a wagon. He borrowed one last year, but the idea of citizenship has budded so that his wants have increased. He wants a wagon all to himself. When an Indian begins to want to accumulate he begins to grow. Tse-kol had sprouted.

"I have no wagon," said Her Majesty, sorrowfully. "I wish I had. The Agent will issue one to you. Go to the Agent."

Tse-kol does not speak English fluently when excited. The words "Go to the Agent" seem to be a red rag to the Nez Perces. Tse-kol falls violently into the vernacular, and James, the Interpreter, comes to the rescue of his ideas, and this is a summary of his tale of woe. He had been to the Agent and modestly proffered his request for a Government Wagon. The Agent said there were none left; all were issued. Tse-kol sees a wagon in the Agency yard and asks, "Whose wagon is that?"

"It is *mine*," was the answer.

"What you pay for it?" asks the persistent Tse-kol. "I give money. You give wagon. I buy it."

"No," says the Agent, "I gave it to Pah-kos."

"All right," says Tse-kol, and he goes straight to Pah-kos.

It is news to Pah-kos; he is incredulous; but he goes and demands the wagon. The Agent tells him he is mistaken; he has not given him a wagon. Pah-kos hunts up Tse-kol, who returns with him to establish his own veracity. The Agent "grows red in the face and talks much." The Indians do not gather the gist of his remarks, but they hold on to the wagon idea until finally the Agent says, "Well, I'll give you the wagon for thirty cords of wood."

Pah-kos at first thinks it a fair bargain, but upon consideration finds that thirty cords of wood at six dollars a cord comes to one hundred and eighty dollars, and he and Tse-kol talk it over and strengthen each other's vertebrae and at last Pah-kos tells the Agent that he will not pay wood for the wagon. It is a Government wagon anyhow, and "Washington" does not ask Indians to buy wagons which are already paid for out of tribal money, and it ends with Pah-kos carrying off the wagon, while Tse-kol, left in the lurch, comes to Her Majesty.

"Indians all say Agent give harness, wagons, plows,

every thing, when you come," said he. "When you go, no-body get nothing."

Poor Tse-kol! He had waited our arrival in hope,—a for-lorn hope. A wagon would carry him straight to citizenship. The Allotting Agent touches the mysterious paper lying be-fore her, with nervous fingers and her eyes have a strained look as Tse-kol steps dejectedly out of the room.

It is three P.M. by this time and the foolscap sheet on the table has six lines on it. The Cook counts them as she walks across the floor. The lines have an irregular appearance and she hears the Special Agent mutter, "It is hard to keep a ju-dicial mind."

While the Cook is wondering if her superior officer is en-gaged in some hidden law suit and is writing her own brief, in walks Chumliks, an English speaking Indian, who is also bitten with the insane desire to become a citizen. Her Majesty has a taking way when she talks, and she has talked a good deal during the last three years. It has borne fruit ripe for the harvest. Alas! Where are the reapers? Chumliks is one of those despised "returned students," who wants to be a citizen so much that he has worked steadily on his land for three years, ever since it was run out for him by the Surveyor. He has a fine field of wheat and he comes to ask advice. The Agent drives his buggy right through his wheat field every time he goes to town, and all the Agency employees do the same. He says the road must go that way. Chumliks has fenced the field and left bars across the road. It is too much trouble to put up the bars, and so the cattle get in and ruin his wheat.

It is dinner-time before Chumliks' story is told, and he goes away comforted by the promise that the Surveyor shall be sent to see what can be done towards making a new road. As Chumliks goes out the school band strikes up "In the Sweet By and By" and the happy boys and girls march past the house, training for the 4th of July procession. We all go out and look at the pleasant sight and rejoice that we are de-scendants of the signers of the Declaration of Independence.

"I am glad," says the Cook, "that I have a realizing sense that 'all men are born free and equal.'" She is standing in the

159

rays of the afternoon sun; the grass is greener than usual, the air less full of alkali dust, the cottonwood trees along the creek are fresh in new foliage and "every prospect pleases"; and yet the Cook sighs as she watches the evolutions of the little company of children, and while she is still gazing at what she has ceased to see, the door opens behind her and a "blanket Indian" goes softly in.

Isa–isa–har–lyk is a perfectly reliable Indian, a good worker, and ambitious to be a citizen. He has the reputation in the tribe of a "straight" Indian,—one that speaks the truth. He is young: were he white, he would be called an enterprising young man. If he could express himself in English with as much imagination as he has directness of speech in the Nez Perce, any little extra length of his black locks and any low-necked dress he might affect would be set down to the exigencies of a practical nature and would not count against his honesty of purpose. He has come to relate some of the difficulties to his line of march towards "citizenship" and "equal rights before the law."

He had the misfortune, to start with, of an allotment which was claimed by a white man for his wife and family on the plea that said wife was a Nez Perce. He failed to prove his claim and the tribe refused to adopt the family on account of their bad character. He was *ordered* off the Reservation, but he pursued the line of tactics which has proved eminently successful in similar cases. He refused to go and sat down upon the land and put in a crop of potatoes, etc., which he gathered in the Fall and distributed among the Indians after the most approved campaign fashion. The Agent issued wire for fencing to another white man, whose wife was entitled to an allotment and this white man *lent* it to Box. (Box was the interloper's name.) He remained in undisturbed possession, until the Department at Washington made some inquiries. Then the Agent reported Box as *removed*. "He had not been on the Reservation since December." Isa–isa–har–lyk says he has never been off at all and that he has planted again this spring, has plowed and sowed a part of his, Isa–isa–har–lyk's, land.

"What is the crop?" asked Her Majesty.

"Barley."

"Is your allotment fenced?"

"Not that piece Box has planted."

"Why not?"

"Box says if I fence that he or I must die."

"Tell me the exact words."

"He said he would lock horns with me."

"Have you been to see the Agent about this?"

"Yes."

"Well?"

"Agent said 'Box was *not on the Reservation*,'" and the Indian smiled. "Perhaps," he added, "now you have come back he will go off for a few days. Indians all say when they see the back of your head things go straight,—when you go out of sight, much trouble; every body have sore heart."

The Allotting Agent sits very still, one hand resting on the sheet of foolscap paper before her, and looks wistfully at Isa–isa–har–lyk. The Cook catches the glance. "Go home," said she to the Indian. "Take up Box's fence carefully and lay it outside your line, and set your own fence down good and strong: when the barley is ripe, cut it and feed it to your horses. If Box troubles you in any way come directly to *me*. I, at least, am a free and independent citizen of the United States of America, with the privilege of free speech, if not of a vote and, as I live, I'll find a way out for you."

The Indian lays his small hand, which is hardened with work, in hers and says, "A-ah," and goes out and Ah-kah comes in. He is one of the little band of Christian Indians, of irreproachable character and industrious habits. He wants wire fencing; has been to the Agent, who tells him there is no more wire and there will be no more issued. Ah-kah is in despair. He thinks wire fencing the direct line to citizenship, and he wants it badly. "No use plow," says he. "White men's cattle thick like crickets. No wire, no fields."

"Logical, for an Indian," says the Cook. "Where has all the wire gone, Ah-kah?"

"Wa-tue-tsue-wa-tsa" (I don't know), says Ah-kah. "Lots of Indians can't get wire."

"Wa-tue-tsue-wa-tsa," repeats Her Majesty as Ah-kah

passes disconsolately out into the unsympathetic world. Who cares whether or no the longing in him shall ever be appeased by fruition or crushed into despair?

By this time there were eight lines on the fateful sheet and Her Majesty had taken a new pen and dipped it in the ink when Te-le-pah appeared at the open window. He wears a linen coat, always clean, a white felt hat, and looks not unlike a strolling Methodist preacher. Te-le-pah raises strawberries and other fruits that will grow on his land.

Last year we had peaches from him that were as big as walnuts and as hard, but it was a dry season. He says that the berries are a failure this spring, but the peaches promise well. Te-le-pah is a good worker and knows how to manage. He has a pronounced talent for building fences, has the whole of his allotment fenced, cañons and all, and the wire between some of his posts is as perpendicular as a kite-string. He has also a long tongue in his head, and has succeeded by its skillful employment, in drawing his full share of plows, hammers, wagons, etc., from the Agent. More ability to talk would be an advantage to the Indian in general. Some people are afraid to talk because, when one talks a good deal, one sometimes tells the truth. Te-le-pah looked in at the window now as if he had something to say.

"What is it?" asked Her Majesty, and then we all went out on the porch, for we knew that, once started, Te-le-pah would have his say and fresh air was requisite to stimulate our powers of endurance. The Special Agent's forehead was corrugated and the white hairs on her head shone in the glare of the Idaho sun, and her eyes had a far away look as Te-le-pah rambled on. I am not going to tell his tale as he told it, but only a bit of it as a fair sample of it all. This is not made up of fancy sketches, but of plain, unvarnished truth: every story told is proved fact.

Te-le-pah said he had come to get some information. He expected to be a citizen before long and wanted to be posted as to his *rights before the law*. How long did we think it would be before the Indians would be allowed to take care of their own business? "Wa-tue-tsue-wa-tsa," said the Cook, and Te-le-pah went on to say that he was troubled about a scheme to lease a part of the Indian's land to white stockmen, which the Agent was pressing upon the tribe. He said he thought there was a "colored gentleman in the fence"—that was about the English of his remark, but he put it in more elegant Nez Perce. Because, said he, there are fifteen thousand head of cattle *now* on the Reservation, for which no price is paid, and why should anybody want to lease land, the benefit of which they can get for nothing?

True, oh, Te-le-pah, a logical conclusion, if you *are* an Indian. He went on to tell us that there had been a great council of the tribe, lasting three days, to consider this lease, and that the Indians had unanimously voted against it. Their consent could never be gained but the Agent was not pleased and Te-le-pah suspected that "Washington" would never know how the Indians felt about the matter.

"Bad, very bad! everything go wrong this winter," said Te-le-pah, and the man spoke the truth.

The tract described in the lease was one Her Majesty had allotted two years ago. It was covered with Indian farms, orchards and homes. Nothing but cañons and rough basaltic formations remained, and the terms of the lease were such that, if acceded to, the entire Reservation would be practically opened to cattle and no Indian farming possible. The Agent said that it was very "important politically" to get the consent of the tribe to this scheme: that "Washington" wanted it; but the Indians were firm in their refusal. Not a man voted in favor of it, and now they are afraid some trick will be played upon them; that, in spite of their attitude, they will wake up some day and find themselves sold.

"A few of the Agency Indians will be induced to sign a paper, and it will be sent on to Washington," said Te-le-pah, "and that will count more than all the council."

Right again, oh, Te-le-pah. Gossip as you are, you have a prophetic soul in your red skin.

"We are afraid," said he. "Agent works with white men all time."

"Te-le-pah," said the Cook, "The Indians must learn to take care of themselves. Nobody else will. You must stop quarrelling among yourselves and combine against—against," the Cook stops aghast. What is she saying? Against *what*, against *whom*, must the Indians combine if they would be saved?

Te-le-pah waits to hear.

"Against *traitors!*" says the Cook, and she walks off across the school-grounds to the board shanty where the little intrepid missionary lives, the woman whose Christ-like life is a miracle in this land.

Te-le-pah says "A-ah" and walks thoughtfully out of the gate and mounts his little dappled pony and a cloud of dust marks his road up the valley and Her Majesty sits down at her table before the still unexplained paper. She crosses her hands upon it, and bows her head upon her hands and the four bare walls of the room shut out the glint of the sunlight on the lowest trees, the tint of the blossoms on the hills and the singing of birds. . . .

* * *

Letter Twenty-Seven

Lapwai
September 6th, 1892

You have cause for your complaint of my long silence. None of us have written many letters this year. The season now drawing to a close has not been prolific of pleasant themes and our endeavor has been to refrain from dwelling upon much that has been forced upon our observation. The silences are eloquent, could you but read them.

When Her Majesty has gathered up the few remaining loose ends of her work and the last belated aspirant to citizenship has been taken under the aegis of the Constitution and the Law, we shall gladly turn our faces towards the East, bringing with us the fine, rich, red hue of the Indian complexion and his love of unmixed nature, with the healthy appetite of the coyote and the eagle's intolerance of a cage. What will you do with us when the spring buds burst open and the wild spirit wakes? Will you lift your roof and let us lie under the stars?

My last letter from this side of the Rockies is to you, as was my first, four years ago. These four years! How long and how short the perspective, varying as do our points of view. . . .

But, long or short, those years have left their mark upon us all: how deep and lasting the impression, we have yet to learn. On the surface, Her Majesty has developed a few lines across her fair forehead; the Cook and the Photographer have less self reliance and more knowledge than they started out with; life is not so big a joke as it used to be to any of us; we do not laugh as much and Briggs smokes more; the little spring that was in the spirit of our faithful interpreter seems to have lost its tension and we can no longer call Dick and Jimmy young horses.

There have been changes also in our environment.

Officials have come and gone; some bad, others better, and some worse, and the Indians have accommodated themselves to each as best they could, as best they must, finding in all only their typical white man, just as the white man picks out his ideal savage with the isolated unbalanced point of a few individuals.

And the Nez Perces themselves in these four years, though slow to change, have not been altogether superior to the logic of events, or indifferent to gentler influences. There is John Allen, for instance, who, when we first arrived within his horizon, refused to speak to us, turned from our friendly advances with a noble scorn; but, a year later, begged to "take our hand" and ever since has been our fast friend, with the confidence of a child in our good will towards himself in particular and towards his tribe in general.

Then there is Utzen Mallican, the old chief, one of the leading obstructionists, who, though he had never committed an overt act against Her Majesty, must have entertained a lively animosity, since he recently expressed so great a satisfaction at having been allowed to live long enough to repent.

"What if I had died hating the 'Measuring Woman,'" he said one day when he had come to see us at Lapwai, on our return from the East.

He was as gentle as he was dignified, with a serene smile on his rugged features as he strove to make us understand how changed a man he was.

And there have been changes, slight but significant, in the management of the Indians. The school for the youngest children which was located at the Agency and under the direct care and influence of the Agent, has been incorporated with that at Lapwai under the supervision of Mr. McConville, and in a competition for the privilege of building and operating a new ferry over the Clearwater River, a white man lost and an Indian won. This is an immense concession, but do not jump to the conclusion that Indians, though now nascent citizens of the United States, can be trusted to oversee their own affairs in any great measure. They are still wards, and for twenty-five years, must continue to be "managed." Indian capital and Indian brain must yet wait a quarter of a century for the white man's freedom to expand.

* * *

Later, Genesee, Sept. 13th

Yesterday was not an easy day for any of us, for we were taking our last look at our red friends and they clustered about us in a mute, pathetic way, hard to see unconcerned. Miss Kate hovered about among them with now and then a word in Nez Perce, bringing always the responsive "A-ah," and all day long we walked softly about our household cares, with always some unspeakable emotion underneath the commonest word.

Early in the morning James' grandmother came to see us. She had ridden Checopath over the snow covered mountains all the way from Kamiah to bid us good bye and to bring us the parting gift of a tanned coyote skin, all she possessed in this world that she *could* give as an expression of her love for the stranger who had understood her a little and had recognized her as a child of the same One, All Father.

As she stood shivering in the frosty air, a thin shawl drawn about her shrunken shoulders, James grew more and more distressed until at last he said, "It is not our fault! We provide plenty of warm clothing, but she gives it all away."

"Yes," said Her Majesty, "I understand. The Indian's ethical standards are quite different from our own. The richest man in the tribe is not he who has accumulated the most wealth, but he who has given away the most."

I wonder . . . if any of us, with all our start in life and the props about us ever since, will ever arrive at the state of sublime patience and self abnegation of a righteous Indian?

* * *

At last our quarters at Lapwai were swept clean of all traces of our occupancy, the only remaining can of beef had been given away, our bits of furniture disposed of. Dick and Jimmy had been transferred to the ownership of James, whose affection for them would ensure their good treatment. The wagon was given to old Abraham. It would be a help to him, Her Majesty said. He had horses, but could no longer ride and his wife could now take him to his church sometimes and to see Miss Kate, to the comfort of his old age. The Cook said, "Yes, it is a most appropriate way of disposing of that wagon. It would be best appreciated by a blind man."

It now stood before the door and James was putting our trunk into it. In another hour we should be "on the grade" to Genesee, when Miss Kate appeared to tell us that John Allen wished to wave goodbye. Could we see him?

"Yes, certainly," said Her Majesty.

"Then I'll bring him in."

She returned in a few moments with John and after the usual little courtesys of leave-taking, the man still lingered as if loath to go and finally Miss Kate said, "John has something to say."

"What is it," asked Her Majesty.

"He wants to know if you are fond of wild animals."

The Special Agent hesitated a moment; then, thinking that perhaps she might fall in John's estimation if she made an unqualified confession of her sentiments regarding wild animals, she said yes, she was fond of looking at the animals in cages at the Zoo.

"He says do you like to sit on them?" continued Miss Kate.

Now this was asking a great deal of Her Majesty. She really could not go on prevaricating in the very presence of a Missionary and she could not tell a direct falsehood even to an Indian. It was embarrassing and John stood anxiously waiting for her reply. With a sudden inspiration she said, well, yes, if it were *dead*; she would not mind sitting on a wild animal, if it was necessary to be done.

"A-ah," said John, and he went out with alacrity, to return in a few moments with a beautiful cougar skin, which, beaming with luminous satisfaction, he presented to Her Majesty. And now, if he had doubted, he must have been convinced of her fondness for wild animals, since she raved over the skin and stroked its glossy fur and admired it to his heart's content. But all the time she was trying to think a way out of the embarrassing situation. John's present was the Indian token of friendship and must be reciprocated: to accept the gift and make no return would dishonor the friendship and what had she to give? Money would not do—one must not pay for a free will offering, and the house was swept bare. John still stood smiling and Miss Kate waited to interpret.

Her Majesty's perplexity at last dawned upon the gentle Missionary, and she said, "John would be delighted to have the rocking chair you gave me."

"But that would not be right."

"Oh, yes, I'll make it right with John."

And so it happened that, as we drove out of the valley, John also climbed the opposite hill with his rocking chair across his pony. It was a gift sure to please his wife who was indeed his better half, and the hidden prop which could account for the uncompromising rigidity of John's backbone in matters of the church where he was a ruling elder, as well as in those of lesser moment, yet which make for general prosperity and progress. John's home was always comfortable and the neatness of Mrs. John above suspicion. I am glad to think of that rocking chair as still another factor in Indian civilization. Anything that keeps him moving, helps.

You will see by the later date of this letter that we are in Genesee, an enterprising little town on a spur of the N.P.R.R. [Northern Pacific Railroad]. In the morning we shall say goodbye to the few friends who have accompanied us thus far and take the train for the East. In the week's journey across the continent we shall have time to review the outcome of our earnest endeavors, so far as it has been revealed to us. But if it has been well for us, and well for the Indian, that Her Majesty and not another should have been sent to the Nez Perce tribe, is not for us to know. We can only leave the question among the unsolvable, whose multitude grows ever greater as life goes on.

As for what we have learned of value to ourselves or to our generation, it may not count for much. No isolated experience counts for much, only, as a thread in the warp and woof, it helps to make the pattern.

I said something like this to the Cook as we were warming our stiffened fingers at the hotel fire in the cold of the evening and Her Majesty was writing some last bit of business paper at the table near by. There was a far away look in the eyes of the Cook as she asked, "Do you remember the old pine tree at one of our first camps? The one the Surveyor cut into?"

"The bearing tree? Oh, yes."

"And the Indian that sat on his pony and watched?" "Yes, old Simon."

"The picture," said the Cook, "is before me now. I wish I could paint it. Did it never occur to you that the Indian was like that bearing tree? Just look at that old gnarled fellow on his pony, rough and seamed by wind and frost and rain, with the scowl of the elements on his face. Barbarian, we call him, and Heathen, and yet, they who would establish a line to God's Kingdom must needs stop and look and wonder at the Indian. There is something in the man that will not let us pass him by without especial notice. What is it in the picture of old Simon, sitting dumb upon his pony, gazing solemnly at the cut in the bearing tree, that makes it indelible to me? I wish I knew."

You see, my dear N., that, though each step in life *may* bring a bit of added knowledge, it must leave an accumulation of mystery. But this is the Indian that we are glad to carry away with us; not the "bloody savage" of the soldier sent to fight him; not the "thieving rascal" of the borderman who preys upon him; not the "dirty dog" of the traveller who encounters the ravelled edge of him and draws his garments away from contaminating contact; not the "ignorant creature" to be "managed" by the officials sent to be masters of him; not the interesting curiosity of the "scientific" investigators who analyse and tabulate and make capital of him. *Our* Indian is Miss Kate's Indian. Still something of a riddle, but partially unlocked by the key of loving kindness. The Old Billy who chopped the ceiling of his house to pieces to make coffins for the people who died during a pestilence; the Utzen Mallican who had the manliness to begin a new life in his old age; the John Allen with his steadfast faith in God and his friends; the blind Abraham who sees his duty and does it without the help of his eyes; Felix the gentleman, and Robert the martyr, with Luke and James and John, apostles to the Lemhi country,[29] and a host of others, with a multitude of women, all with their faces set toward the East, waiting for the breaking of the day that will open to them a fair chance, though it should be but the day of their death.

* * *

The noises of the hotel have one by one been stilled. Her Majesty has tied the last bit of red tape needed at this end of her work. We have all said goodbye to Dick and Jimmy, faithful horses, and to James, their faithful driver. They will go back to Lapwai before we wake in the morning, though we, too, must start early. My bed waits for me, but there is, I know not what, reluctance to losing myself in sleep; as if it were to be a final letting go of all I have known here. I throw the window wide open and there are the stars. Oh, how friendly the stars have become! Will they ever look down upon me again through a tent opening? Shall I ever again live face to face with Mother Nature? Or must the clearer insight into life's mysteries which has come to my unobstructed vision, fade and be lost in the confusing complexities of conventional living?

With a sense of coming loss, I strain my eyes to catch a glimpse of the horizon line over the Nez Perce land, but I see nothing—, only the stars. And the stars I can see in Washington: the same stars that the Indians see; and there is but one sun, and one Father over all—and I close the window and say goodnight.

Writer's Note

As we have reviewed in these pages, there have walked beside us, hand in hand with the ghosts of the past, the actualities of the present, and double pictures have met us all along the way.

We could not today pitch our tent here, there and everywhere upon the Indian land, and lie down to sleep with perfect confidence in the protecting power of the three tape fastenings of our door flap, nor might we ride, unarmed and ungarded, all over the Nez Perce country as we did a dozen years ago; for the white man has entered the land, with pickaxe and plough and pistols.

Our old grazing grounds are tormented by harrow and spade, wire fences criss-cross our wagon trails; and where the Photographer washed his negatives in the crystal Clearwater, the Chinaman stands with pan and shovel and frets the golden sands. The puma's lair is disturbed, for miners burrow into the mountains and prospecters haunt the cañons, and in all the vale of Kamiah there is no longer the unbroken peace of nature or the unthinking rest of man; for the Reservation has been opened, the tribe has been scattered and, thanks to the prescience of Her Majesty, the red man is separated from his white neighbor only by the breadth of his own allotment.

The Indian carpenter builds the cabin for the white settler who in turn breaks the Indian's land on shares; Post offices have been established and neighborhood schools have depleted the Government institution: churches have multiplied and town sites are laid out at the crossings of the old pony trails and on the upland where we camped with Hannah and Maria is a city named for Her Majesty.

A sturdy little steamboat ploughs its way to the head of navigation on the Clearwater and takes away the grain from the warehouse of James Stuart, our ci-devant driver and interpreter and the echo of its parting salute is caught and prolonged by the shriek of the incoming locomotive.

Felix owns and operates a lucrative ferry over the Clearwater and a gristmill in the town of Stuart, which has sprung up on the allotment of a Nez Perce widow; and his son, home from Carlisle, keeps a store and advertises largely in the newspaper of the place; and where old Isaac paddled our boat over the rocks and sands of the South Fork, spans a substantial iron bridge.

Robert's voice is no longer heard in the little church and Billy treads softly in another "God's house," but the bell he rang still peals out over the disturbed valley and a younger Nez Perce preaches to red and white man alike and native missionaries still go out to carry the tidings of peace and fellowship to the Lemhi and Shoshones as, long ago, in urgency of the same spirit, their fathers carried the calumet to make brothers and sons in alien tribes.

At Lapwai, where also the rumbling locomotive jars the cadence of Nez Perce hymns, Miss Kate still lives, in a house now, beautiful and holy, to which many well-trodden paths lead and from which radiates in undimmed lustre that influence which has made the Nez Perce tribe so signal an example of progress in civilization.

Where the Indians at Lapwai camped at their Tal-lik-lykt festival, they hold now, at the Fourth of July, a gospel meeting, and from the tents back of Miss Kate's new home, instead of war songs, hymns of prayer and praise echo through the valley.

As I write here in Washington, comes James Stuart, President of the Board of Trade of the town of Stuart, with Joe Kentuck . . . typical Indian, influential Nez Perce. They come as a "delegation," on business with the Government. They do not seek audience of the "Great Father," to orate upon their fallen estate and beg for redress of real or fancied wrongs—not they! They go straight to the Capitol and call upon the Idaho Senators: they are American citizens and their rights are guaranteed by their votes.

And lastly, to prove that pessimism hath no right to be in a moving world where one can always *wait*, there is no longer an Agent to "manage" the Nez Perces. And now, with tribal bonds broken away and the individual man standing more and more responsible for his own future, we may hopefully leave our Indian friends to work out their own salvation.

AT HOME, *January, 1904*

Notes

Preface

1. The Nez Perce tribe has published the first volume of a projected two-volume history. See Allen Slickpoo, *Noon Nee-Me-Poo (We, the Nez Perces)* (Lapwai, Idaho: The Nez Perce Tribe of Idaho, 1973). Another important study is Deward E. Walker, Jr., *Conflict and Schism in Nez Perce Acculturation: A Study of Religion and Politics* (Pullman, Wash.: Washington State University Press, 1968).

Introduction

1. C. C. Painter, *The Dawes Land in Severalty Bill and Indian Emancipation* (Philadelphia, 1887), p. 5; *Annual Report of the Commissioner of Indian Affairs*, 1887, p. 4. Hereafter the annual reports of the commissioners of Indian affairs will be cited as *ARCIA* with the date. All of the citations to commissioners' reports refer to the separately bound department editions rather than to the versions included in House Executive Documents (the two versions vary primarily in pagination).

2. Meriwether Lewis, *The Expedition of Lewis and Clark*, 2 vols., March of American Facsimile Series, no. 56 (Ann Arbor, Mich.: University Microfilms, 1966), 2:293.

3. For descriptions of the separation of Nez Perce villages and the impact of their social organization on tribal politics, see Herbert J. Spinden, "The Nez Perce Indians," *Memoirs of the American Anthropological Association* 2, pt. 3 (November 1908); Edward S. Curtis, *The North American Indian*, 20 vols. (Seattle: E. S. Curtis, 1907–30), 8:41–53; Verne F. Ray, "Cultural Relations in the Plateau of Northwestern America," *Publications of the Frederick Webb Hodge Anniversary Publications Fund*, vol. 3 (Los Angeles, 1939); Francis Haines, *The Nez Perce, Tribesmen of the Columbia Plateau* (Norman: University of Oklahoma Press, 1955), chap. 2; Alvin M. Josephy, *The Nez Perce Indians and the Opening of the Northwest* (New Ha-

ven: Yale University Press, 1965), chap. 1; Walker, *Conflict and Schism*, chap. 2; Sven Liljeblad, *The Idaho Indians in Transition* (Pocatello, Idaho: Idaho State University Museum, 1972); and Deward Walker, Jr., *Indians of Idaho*, Anthropological Monographs of the University of Idaho (Moscow, Idaho, 1973), p. 12.

4. Lewis, *The Expedition of Lewis and Clark*, 2:293.

5. Quoted in Walker, *Conflict and Schism*, p. 42.

6. For a detailed description of the treaty negotiations and their aftermath, see Josephy, *The Nez Perce Indians*, chaps. 8, 10.

7. Walker gives the most recent account of the Nez Perce dreamer cult (*Conflict and Schism*, pp. 48–53). Other versions appear in Haines, *The Nez Perce*, pp. 193–94, and Helen Addison Howard, *Saga of Chief Joseph* (Caldwell, Idaho: Caxton Printers, 1971), pp. 84–87.

8. Quoted in Josephy, *The Nez Perce Indians*, p. 630.

9. *ARCIA*, 1877, p. 80.

10. Ibid., 1879, p. 57.

11. Ibid., 1893, p. 139.

12. U.S. Senate, *Agreement with the Nez Perce Indians*, Senate Exec. Doc. 31, 53d Cong., 2d sess. (1893), p. 40.

13. Walker, *Conflict and Schism*, p. 77.

14. *ARCIA*, 1911, p. 152.

15. Ibid., 1906, p. 217.

16. For the modern history of the Nez Perces and their political system, see Robert James Riley, "The Nez Perce Struggle for Self Government: A History of Nez Perce Governing Bodies, 1842–1960" (M.A. thesis, University of Idaho, 1961), chaps. 3–6; Slickpoo, *Noon Nee-Me-Poo*, pp. 223–75; and Deward E. Walker, Jr., "Some Limitations of the Renascence Concept in Acculturation: The Nez Perce Case," in *American Indians Today*, ed. Nancy O. Lurie and Stuart Levine (Baltimore: Penguin, 1970).

17. E. B. Borden, "Visit with Miss Jane Gay Dodge, '04," September 19, 1951, MS, Schlesinger Library, Radcliffe College; Jane Gay Dodge to E. B. Borden, May 25, 1952, ibid.

18. Jane Gay Dodge, "Brief Biography of E. Jane Gay," MS, Schlesinger Library.

19. J. Kirkpatrick Flack, *Desideratum in Washington: The Intellectual Community in the Capital City, 1870–1900* (Cambridge, Mass.: Schenkman Publishing Co., 1975), p. 19.

20. Diary for 1888, Papers of Alice C. Fletcher and Francis La Flesche, National Anthropological Archives, Smithsonian Institution, Washington, D.C.

21. For biographical information on Alice C. Fletcher, see Thurman Wilkins, "Alice Cunningham Fletcher," in *Notable American Women, 1607–1950*, ed. Edward T. and Janet James (Cambridge, Mass.: Belknap Press of Harvard University Press, 1971), pp. 630–33; Nancy O. Lurie, "Women in Early American Anthropology," in *Pioneers of American Anthropology*, ed. June Helm (Seattle: University of Washington Press, 1966),

pp. 31–81; and Joan T. Mark, *Four Anthropologists: An American Science in Its Early Years* (New York: Science History Publications, 1980), chap. 3.

22. See, for example, "Sun Dance of the Ogallala Sioux," *Proceedings of the American Association for the Advancement of Science* 31 (1883): 580–84; "Observations on the Laws and Privileges of the Gens in Indian Society," ibid. 32 (1884): 395–96; "Observations upon the Usage, Symbolism and Influence of the Sacred Pipes of Friendship among the Omahas," ibid. 33 (1885): 615–17. Fletcher published descriptions of five Indian ceremonies in the *Sixteenth Annual Report of the Peabody Museum* (1884), pp. 260–333.

23. Alice C. Fletcher, *Indian Education and Civilization*, Special Report, U.S. Bureau of Education, Department of the Interior (Washington, D.C., 1888).

24. The Omaha photographs are included in the E. Jane Gay collection at the Idaho Historical Society. Several of them show a man, probably Francis La Flesche, demonstrating skin scraping and other technics. Some Omaha photographs were included in the original *Choup-nit-ki* volumes but have been omitted here. See also Alice C. Fletcher to F. W. Putnam, November 18, 1888, F. W. Putnam Papers, Harvard University Archives.

25. Jane Gay did most of her photographing with a view camera on a tripod which took five-by-seven-inch and five-by-eight-inch glass plates. The camera was a solid instrument but was by no means the best available. It lacked a shutter, and so to make an exposure Jane Gay had to remove and replace the lens cap, necessitating an exposure time of at least two seconds—not fast enough to stop any action. Longer exposures she timed with a watch. She also had an amateur's hand camera, probably the No. 2 Kodak, introduced in October 1889, which took circular pictures three and one-half inches in diameter on celluloid roll film. (Personal communication from Christopher S. Johnson.)

26. After the death of Maizie Crawford, niece of Sue and Kate McBeth, the collection went to Dr. Francis M. Haines, who gave it to the Idaho State Historical Society (1963 Accession Book, Idaho State Historical Museum, Boise).

27. Slickpoo, *Noon Nee-Me-Poo*, pp. 209–10.

28. Allen and Eleanor Morrill, "Talmaks," *Idaho Yesterdays* 8, no. 3 (Fall 1964): 2–15, report that one missionary lady watched the "heathen" through a pair of glasses and two Presbyterians sneaked out to get a closer look.

29. *Morning Star* 7 (June 1887): 1–2.

30. "Miss Fletcher's Letter from Winnebago Agency," *Red Man* 8 (February 1888): 1–2; "Among the Nez Perces," ibid. 9 (September 1889): 1.

31. "My Dear Capt. Pratt," *Red Man* 9 (November 1889): 5–6.

32. Letters 2, 3, and 5 appeared in *Red Man* 9 (November 1889): 5–6, and ibid. 10 (April 1890): 2–3, 6–7; Letters 7–13 were published in ibid. 10 (December 1890–January 1891): 1–3, (April–May 1891): 6–7, (June 1891): 6–7, and ibid. 11 (July–August 1891): 6–7, (September–October 1891):

5–7, and (November 1891): 6–7; Letter 14 appeared in ibid. 10 (July–August 1890):3.

33. Alice C. Fletcher to Commissioner of Indian Affairs, December 26, 1889, Papers of Alice C. Fletcher and Francis LaFlesche, National Anthropological Archives.

34. Alice C. Fletcher to F. W. Putnam, August 2, 1889, and September 20, 1889, Peabody Museum Papers, Harvard University Archives.

35. See A. C. Fletcher, "Phonetic Alphabet of the Winnebago Indians," *Proceedings of the American Association for the Advancement of Science* 38 (1890): 354–57; A. C. Fletcher with Francis La Flesche and John C. Fillmore, "A Study of Omaha Indian Music," *Papers of the Peabody Museum of Archaeology and Ethnology* 1 (1893): 237–87.

36. Alice C. Fletcher to F. W. Putnam, September 28, 1890, Peabody Museum Papers.

37. See "Ethnological Gleanings among the Nez Perces" (MS, Papers of Alice C. Fletcher and Francis La Flesche, National Anthropological Archives), which includes the life story of an old Nez Perce woman, Nancy, and descriptions of the "whippers" who punish children and of war and hunting incidents, mortuary customs, war customs, and tribal pipes.

38. Kate C. McBeth, *The Nez Perces since Lewis and Clark* (New York: Fleming H. Revell, 1908), p. 239; see also A. C. Fletcher, "Nez Perce Country" (abstract), *Proceedings of the American Association for the Advancement of Science* 40 (1892): 357. A "Map of the Nez Perce Country," drawn by Jonathan "Billy" Williams, 1891, and Alice C. Fletcher's description of the map, MS, are in the National Anthropological Archives.

39. Jane Gay Dodge to E. B. Borden, December 3, 1951, and December 4, 1951, Schlesinger Library.

40. *The Hako: A Pawnee Ceremony*, Twenty-second Annual Report of the Bureau of American Ethnology (Washington, D.C., 1904); *The Omaha Tribe*, Twenty-seventh Annual Report of the Bureau of American Ethnology (Washington, D.C., 1911).

41. Jane Gay Dodge, "Sketch of My First Meeting with Alice C. Fletcher in 1888," MS, 1939, Schlesinger Library.

42. Jane Gay Dodge, "Reminiscences," typed from notes taken by E. B. Borden on a visit to Jane Gay Dodge, December 3, 1951, Schlesinger Library; Jane Gay Dodge to E. B. Borden, November 19, 1952, ibid.

43. Elizabeth Sturge, *Reminiscences of My Life and Some Account of the Children of William and Charlotte Sturge and the Sturge Family of Bristol* (privately printed, 1928), pp. 142–48.

The Letters

Except where otherwise indicated, the information in the following notes was drawn from the following sources: Individuals from the pre-1877 history of the tribe could usually be identified from Alvin Josephy's excellent

The Nez Perce Indians and the Opening of the Northwest. The works cited above by Francis Haines, Helen Addison Howard, Allen Slickpoo, and Herbert J. Spinden were also useful in identifying people and events. For the last two decades of the nineteenth century, the *Annual Reports* of the commissioner of Indian affairs and the proceedings of the 1893 agreement negotiations (contained in *Agreement with the Nez Perce Indians,* cited above) provided a wealth of names and information. Kate McBeth's *The Nez Perces since Lewis and Clark* (cited above) and Mary Crawford's *The Nez Perce Indians since Spalding* (Berkeley, Calif.: Professional Press, 1936) were the principal sources for the background material on people who were connected with the Presbyterian mission. Finally, Erwin Thompson's *Spalding Area: Nez Perce National Historical Park, Idaho* (Denver: National Park Service, 1972) provided important information on the last years of the reservation era.

1. Lewiston, located on the south side of the Clearwater River near its junction with the Snake, was on the Nez Perce Reservation when it became a supply depot for the Idaho miners in 1861. Ignoring treaty guarantees and the protests of many Indians, sternwheelers, teamsters, and enterprising ferrymen began unloading their goods in May of that year. By midsummer the newly named town boasted a population of five thousand. The 1863 treaty altered the reservation's boundaries to account for this and other land seizures.

2. Five people held the post of Nez Perce agent during 1889. Some turnover was to be expected, since the Republicans had squeaked back into the White House the previous fall and such positions were part of the prize. But competition for the post was exacerbated by the campaign of the previous agent, Charles Monteith, to regain his position. Monteith had served from 1882 until 1886, when he had been dismissed in the aftermath of a conflict between tribal factions. Monteith had a great deal of experience on the reservation (he had assisted his brother John when he had been the Nez Perce agent from 1871 to 1879), but his tolerance of traditional lifeways and his willingness to deal with non-Christian leaders angered both the missionaries and the Indians who followed them. Alice Fletcher's ties to these groups must have identified her as one of his enemies. Monteith received his new appointment on July 1, 1889 (the day Alice Fletcher and her group left for Kamiah), but served for only a few months. He resigned when the agency school was placed under a separate administration and its new superintendent turned out to be a political enemy.

3. Fletcher's interpreter was James Stuart, a consistent ally of the "treaty faction" on the reservation. He opposed the hostiles in 1877, even though his wife, Harriet, had been among the group of Joseph's followers that had returned to Lapwai in 1885. She had probably been a child during the war. Stuart remained loyal to Fletcher and the government; he supported the 1893 surplus land sale that completed the allotment process and

in later years he served as a judge in the Court of Indian Offenses. In 1923, when the tribe formed a modern council, James Stuart was its first president.

4. Edward McConville commanded a company of Idaho volunteers in the early stages of the 1877 conflict. His unit included a number of Nez Perce scouts from the treaty faction. When the Fort Lapwai Indian school and the agency were separated into two jurisdictions, McConville became the school's first superintendent.

5. Indian policemen and judges were a regular feature of reservation life in the late nineteenth century. Both groups were appointed by the local agent and were responsible for maintaining law and order in the tribe. From the government's point of view, Indian policemen and judges were both a practical necessity and an integral part of its assimilation program, for it was thought that they would teach their fellow Indians to obey written law and to adopt "civilized" habits. For a detailed account of this aspect of American Indian history, see William T. Hagan, *Indian Police and Judges: Experiments in Acculturation and Control* (New Haven: Yale University Press, 1966).

6. In the version of this letter printed in the Carlisle Indian school newspaper (the *Red Man*), Gay wrote that the reservation was "one hundred miles long and wide." See vol. 9 no. 11 (November 1889): 5.

7. Chulsum Moxmox, also called Yellow Buffalo Bull or Yellow Bull, was a leading member of White Bird's band of nontreaty Nez Perces. His son, Sarpsis Ilppilp, was a member of the raiding party that initiated the 1877 fighting and was killed as Joseph's people retreated across Montana. Yellow Bull was evidently one of those allowed to return to the reservation from Indian Territory in 1885, although Kate McBeth claimed that he came to Lapwai from Colville only to receive an allotment. Yellow Bull's wife may have been a shaman.

8. James Reuben was the son of Reuben, the traditional headman at a village near the present site of Lewiston, Idaho. The elder Reuben was Joseph's brother-in-law, but his attitude toward whites was far different from that of his famous kinsman. In the gold rush of the early 1860s Reuben carried on an active trade with prospectors, even going so far as to build a warehouse to stockpile his merchandise. Despite his father's pliant attitude, James Reuben maintained good relations with his uncle Joseph and the anti-treaty party. The young man acted as an intermediary between the hostiles and General Howard, and made several trips to the Wallowa valley to plead the government's case. And after the fighting was over, James Reuben traveled first to Indian Territory, where he established a day school for the children of the imprisoned renegades, and then to Washington, where he lobbied for their release. In 1883 he won permission for widows of warriors to return, and in 1885 he was successful in gaining the freedom of the entire group. Although he was an early opponent of allotment, Reuben soon decided that Fletcher's proposal was a practical

solution to the twin problems of white encroachment and Indian poverty. His support was important to the anthropologist, who later wrote that Reuben "is a man of gifts and a man who can be made an instrument of much good to his people" (Alice Fletcher to General Heth, August 28, 1889, Papers of the Indian Rights Association, Letters Received, reel 4 of Microfilm Corporation of America microfilm edition).

9. The mound represents the heart of the monster whose body was chopped up and became the different peoples of the earth. The monster's blood became the first Real People (*Nimipu*), as the Nez Perces called themselves.

10. At the trappers' annual rendezvous in 1834, the missionary Jason Lee noted that one young Nez Perce warrior called the The Bull's Head was constantly trying to sing a popular ballad, "The Hunters of Kentucky." As the merriment progressed, the mountain men took to calling the young man Kentuck. The joke evidently appealed to the Indians as well as to the whites because the boisterous warrior kept the name. Kentuck helped guide the early missionaries over the Rockies and remained loyal to the Christians throughout the crisis following the Whitman massacre. The Kentucky referred to here was either this same man—now in his seventies—or Joseph Kentuck, an outspoken opponent of the 1893 surplus land sale and presumably the old warrior's son.

11. Kipkip Pahlekin (or Eagle or Black Eagle) was one of the four Nez Perces who journeyed to St. Louis in 1831 to secure missionaries for their people. He died before he could return home to Kamiah. A second Kipkip Pahlekin, also from Kamiah, was a prominent headman in the 1840s and 1850s. The man who spoke here had probably inherited both his name and his position from these forebears. He continued to oppose allotment and worked to defeat the 1893 surplus land sale.

12. Robert Williams was one of three men who in 1879 became the first Nez Perces to be ordained by the McBeths' Presbyterian mission. Williams had become a student at Sue McBeth's school when it first opened in 1874 and he shared the Presbyterians' opposition to traditional Indian practices. In fact, his work to eradicate the old ways and the favoritism shown him by Sue McBeth led to a split within his congregation and the formation of the Second Presbyterian Church of Kamiah. See Allen Conrad Morrill and Eleanor Dunlop Morrill, *Out of the Blanket: The Story of Sue and Kate McBeth, Missionaries to the Nez Perces* (Moscow, Idaho: University of Idaho Press, 1978).

13. Billy Williams (also called Jonathan or "Business Billy") was one of Kamiah's most successful farmers. He was an early convert to Christianity and had been one of the first elders at the Kamiah church when it was built in 1873.

14. Increasingly during the late nineteenth century, as western states like Idaho entered the Union and began to wield power in Congress, Indian agency appointments were made with the approval of local politi-

cians. This process accelerated during the political upheavals of the 1890s, when Republicans and Democrats scrambled to maintain their standing in a rapidly changing environment.

15. "Mrs. Lawyer" was the wife of Hallalhotsoot, or Lawyer (ca. 1794–1876), a native of Kamiah whose knowledge of English and goodwill toward both mountain men and missionaries had caused him to be recognized by whites as the principal chief of the Nez Perce people. Lawyer was the central figure in the treaty faction and a supporter of the agreements of 1855 and 1863. He had even sold supplies to the miners who invaded the reservation in the early 1860s. According to Mary Crawford (a niece of the McBeths' who joined their mission in 1895), Mrs. Lawyer was with her husband in 1836 when the chief journeyed to the Green River rendezvous site to greet Henry and Eliza Spalding and Marcus and Narcissa Whitman, the first Presbyterian missionaries in the Northwest. Lawyer and his wife were part of the group (which included Kentuck) that guided the two families over the Rockies. In light of her past and the reputation of her husband, it is interesting that Gay believed she was a *tewat* (or *tiwet*), a traditional spiritual leader.

16. Utzen Mallican (or Utsinmalikin) was the name of an important village chief from the Kamiah region who had supported the missionaries and was a member of the Lawyer faction that accepted the 1863 treaty. This first Utsinmalikin died while serving as part of a delegation to Washington, D.C., in 1868. The Utzen Mallican referred to here—perhaps a son who took his father's name—was also a leader in the Kamiah community. He later was reconciled to allotment (see Letter 27, below) and served as a councilman from that area during the negotiations leading to the 1893 land sale.

17. Felix Corbett was related to Robert Williams and was a member of the Kamiah Presbyterian Church. Corbett later became a judge in the Court of Indian Offenses and a supporter of the 1893 land sale.

18. An Indian student band had become a fixture at Carlisle, Haskell, and other large government boarding schools.

19. Although Catholic priests had been in contact with surrounding tribes since the days of the Hudson's Bay Company, the Nez Perce mission had not been established until 1869. The delay was due at least in part to the hostility of Henry Spalding and the early Protestant missionaries, who opposed the "papists" as strenuously as they fought "heathenism." Protestant missionaries also disapproved of the priests' tolerance of long hair and the celebration of traditional ceremonies. Slickpoo mission was a few miles from the agency headquarters, on an upper branch of Lapwai creek.

20. Archie Lawyer was the son of Hallalhotsoot (Lawyer), the principal supporter of the early missionaries and leader of the treaty Nez Perces until his death in 1876. Like Robert Williams, Archie Lawyer had been one of Sue McBeth's first students at her Kamiah mission. Lawyer opposed Joseph and supported the U.S. Army during the 1877 fighting, although he later accompanied James Reuben to Indian Territory and served as a mis-

sionary to the defeated hostiles. He was ordained in 1881. At the end of 1890 (after Gay and Fletcher had returned to the East), Lawyer and his followers raised objections to Robert Williams and his absolute condemnation of old tribal traditions and formed the Second Presbyterian Church of Kamiah. It is significant, however, that Gay saw this split as a conflict between "simple right and justice and godliness" and "the old chiefs." This falling out with Fletcher and the McBeth sisters may have contributed to Lawyer's decision to oppose allotment and argue against the 1893 surplus land sale. For a more detailed discussion of the split among the Kamiah Presbyterians, see Walker, *Conflict and Schism*, pp. 69–70, and A. C. Morrill, *Out of the Blanket*, pp. 232–34, 307–8.

21. Located just outside the southern border of the reservation, Cottonwood was a settlement on the Camas prairie, equidistant from Kamiah and Mt. Idaho. It was the site of one of the nontreaty band's early victories in July 1877.

22. The reference here is to the fur traders' rendezvous, where Indians, white trappers, and merchants from the East met each year for a few weeks of business and revelry. Nez Perces participated in these affairs from about 1811 until they stopped being held in 1840. (Most Nez Perces traded with Americans rather than the British, whom they considered niggardly.) The Indian ceremony which Gay suggests preceded these gatherings was probably the annual camas harvest on the Weippe prairie. There the bands and families that had spent the winter in the isolation of their canyon homes or across the mountains on the northern plains came together for a few weeks of work and fun. The women cooked camas bulbs and formed them into loaves for the winter while the men hunted and eyed each other's ponies. And since this was the largest gathering of Nez Perce people every year, everyone participated in the dancing, horse racing, and trading. Like a number of other tribes, the Nez Perces appear to have practiced serial monogamy. The apparent ease with which tribal members changed mates may have given rise to Gay's vision of wife swapping.

23. Fourteen.

24. Rivalry for control of the annual summer gathering had been going on for over a decade. In 1887 the two groups agreed to hold a joint celebration. Gay's description is of the dissolution of that agreement, and in 1897 the Presbyterians formed the Talmaks Association and began holding their summer encampments on another part of the reservation.

25. Franz Boas, working under the direction of Harvard's F. W. Putnam, was in charge of exhibits in physical anthropology for the World's Columbian Exposition at Chicago in 1893. He sent Fletcher measuring instruments and requested data on the Nez Perces for an exhibit on physical types.

26. See Jonathan "Billy" Williams's Nez Perce map and notes, National Anthropological Archives.

27. Deward Walker has identified a pre-missionary ritual which may correspond to this "sun worship." Walker argues that the Nez Perces had

been devastated by precontact diseases and their traditional lifeways disrupted by European technology. In response the tribe adopted some of the traders' Christian practices in hopes of gaining control over their new situation. See Walker, *Conflict and Schism*, pp. 31–35.

28. According to Slickpoo, *Noon Nee Me Poo*, the names of the four men who went to St. Louis were Ka-ow-poo (Of the Dawn), Ta-weis-se-sim-nihn (Nohorns), Heh-yookts-Toe-nihn (Rabbit Skin Leggings), and Wep-tes-tse-mookh Tse-mookh (Black Eagle).

29. Sue McBeth trained a number of Nez Perce ministers who became missionaries to other tribes. Among them were James Hayes, Mark Williams, and Enoch Pond.

INDEX

188